Angel With A Broken Wing

My Journey into Healing

Disclaimer

This memoir is intended to document important milestones I reached in my life. Any references to actual people and events represents my best recollection and memory. If anyone is offended by these words, please note that they were written only to heal.

Angel With A Broken Wing
My Journey into Healing

Valerie A. Yarborough

Ruggedaisy Press
Milton / WA

Library of Congress Control Number: 2003091217

First Edition, E-book ISBN: 1-4107-2487-5
First Edition, Paperback ISBN: 1-4107-2488-3
First Edition, Dust Jacket ISBN: 1-4107-4435-3
Second Edition, Paperback ISBN: 0-9767317-0-3

Published and distributed by
Ruggedaisy Press
Post Office Box 1953
Milton, WA 98354

To all who were quoted in this book, thank you for your words have enabled me to create an artistry of healing for the world.

Printed in the United States of America
Book design by HyunSook Chung

To All of My Angels on this side of life and the other...

and especially for my father, Baxter "Rugged" Yarborough, for assuring me that "something good will come of this." My brother, John "Big Daddy" Jackson, for being my brother and my dawg, my cousin, Aretta Tilley Hazzard, for showing her love, and my friends Mary Wedel, Brenda Monroe, and Dinah Moninski, Scleroderma victims, who fought with much courage and dignity always looking good despite their pain.

Angel with a Broken Wing

An angel afloat with one broken wing,
Asked God will He help her, if she sings?

She sang out loud for everyone to hear,
Then suddenly her eyes were filled with tears.

With each tear that fell from her face,
She realized that the wing could be replaced.

She stopped her singing and started to pray,
For God to bless her with just one more day.

He answered her prayer and said, "Let it be.
I want this beautiful child to be set free."

When she awoke as the sun began to rise,
She noticed her wing moving from side to side.

She started laughing, then began to cry.
I'm free again. God has let me fly!

She gave God praise for such an amazing grace,
Today she still thanks Him for setting her straight.

Now she knows if it should happen again,
God always answers prayers through thick and thin.

Sharon Brinkley
March 30, 1999

Table of Contents

Table of Contents, cont...

Part One
I Am a Vulture

"In Egypt, the vulture was a mother symbol... enabling other life to sustain itself. For the Pueblo Indians, it was a symbol of purification. In Greek tradition, the vulture was considered to be a descendent of a mythical creature... a symbol of heaven and earth, spirit and matter, guardian and avenger. The king vulture will fly alone or in pairs usually high and far away from others. For those with this totem, it speaks of a coming time when you will be noticed more for what you do than how you appear."
~ from Animal-Speak: The Spirit & Magical Powers of Creatures Great and Small by Ted Andrews

I am a vulture in many ways. As an African American woman and daughter of a bricklayer, I've often been unfairly judged - like the vulture - by the way that I appeared rather than the gifts I could bestow. But it wasn't until my physical body began to fail me when I was diagnosed with Scleroderma (otherwise known as Systemic Sclerosis) in January 1996, that I embarked on a journey towards learning to love and nurture myself, accepting my limitations and seeking new wisdom. Like the vulture, I try to ride the wind bourne updrafts more often and use what is available to me, even if I have to really scavenge. I aspire to the grace and ease of a vulture in flight. Throughout my seven-year journey into healing, I've learned how to flap my wings less like other birds and use the energy of the air current, like vultures do... which freed me from the gravity of my death sentence. Now I often soar effortlessly.

But my journey wasn't easy. It started with a single tear that trickled into a stream, filling a pond, and flowing into a lake that emptied into the Puget Sound and eventually the ocean. I didn't know, when I moved from my lifelong home in Washington, D.C. to the opposite coast in Seattle that vultures prefer forested habitats.

This geographic change was just one of many that I made. My faith in God, and my many special angels have been constant companions on my spiritual, emotional and physical journey into healing. I now believe that there is a divine plan and purpose for my life. But first there were lessons to learn. Pain to feel. Pills to take. Shame to overcome. Tests to pass. Negative habits and beliefs to release. Love to experience. And friendships to nurture. There were apologies to make and songs to sing.

This state of "dis-ease" came to mold me into what God wanted me to be. Just as Tramaine and Walter Hawkins sang in their song, "The Potter's House," God is the potter and I am the clay. I gave Him the fragments of my broken life and body and found love, joy, and healing in the Potter's house.

Everyone suffers from something. If you are suffering, I ask you to remember that it's okay to feel "broken," because only then can God put you back together again. God is a healer. But as humans, I believe we each have to make a choice about whether we want to be healed. God answered my prayer to be healed, but asked much of me along my journey. I often wanted to give up on life ~ and sometimes still do ~ but I trust in the work God asks me to do. I have been amply rewarded. As the song goes, "you don't have to stay in the shape that you're in, because The Potter wants to put you back together again." And if I can do it ~ trust me ~ so can you.

As the first African American to share her story of living with Scleroderma, I invite you to listen and learn.

ABOUT SCLERODERMA

Scleroderma means "hardening of the skin." An estimated 300,000 individuals suffer from localized or Systemic Sclerosis, the worst form of Scleroderma. It is a chronic, degenerative dis-ease that causes the overproduction of collagen in the body's connective tissue. This protein (collagen) is normally responsible for keeping our skin and organs supple. But when it is overproduced, it makes tissue thick and immobile. It is most serious when it affects internal organs, causing severe damage to organs and other complications, while compromising the immune system. There is also a greater incidence of Scleroderma among women.

SYSTEMIC SCLEROSIS

While Scleroderma attacks individuals in unique ways, I had Systemic Sclerosis, the worst form of Scleroderma. It is quickly degenerative and often life threatening. Symptoms include: chronic fatigue, body and muscle pain, Central Nervous System (CNS) vasculitis, joint and dental problems, TMJ (temporomandibular joint, a jaw joint dis-ease), and lung involvement that can create a persistent cough, scarring of the lung tissue, and lower tolerance for movement.

HOW TO GET AN ACCURATE DIAGNOSIS

Diagnosis of Scleroderma may be very difficult, particularly in the early stages of the dis-ease, because many symptoms are common to, or may overlap with those of other dis-eases, especially other connective tissue dis-eases such as rheumatoid arthritis, lupus and polymyositis.

The diagnostic process may require consultations with rheumatologists (arthritis specialists) and dermatologists (skin specialists) as well as blood studies and a variety of specialized tests, depending on which organs are affected.[2]

---

[1] Scleroderma Research Foundation brochure, *The Business of Hope, the Science of Miracles*
[2] Scleroderma Foundation, www.scleroderma.org/fact.html.

Chapter One
The Beginning Of My Journey

"Your talent is God's gift to you. What you do with it is your gift back to God."

~ Unknown

May 1995. Before then, I was a thirty-something year old vocalist, dancer, actress, and voice-over artist (a professional narrator for radio, film, and television) ~ busy in my life like everybody else. I was a college graduate with a background in radio. While I waited to get rich and famous, I made ends meet working as an admissions officer in a busy hospital Emergency Department in Fort Washington, Maryland. In my off hours, I waited for true love to show up.

Imagine being born with a multitude of gifts and talents and enjoying them to the utmost. And then one day, realizing that they had all been stolen, one by one. Scleroderma took my talents and filled me with hurt, disappointment, and shame. When I entered center stage, fully dressed, and ready to perform, the lights were darkened by dis-ease. There was no music. And my body could only move to the lethargic rhythm of arthritis and lung dis-ease. No microphone waited to catch the strains of magical melodies slipping from my lips to bless a waiting ear. No camera was poised to capture the essence of a specially groomed character for this feature film. Until I lost my gifts, I had no idea how incredible I was. I could sing, dance, act, read, write and voice commercials. I was talented but adrift.

Seven years ago, this chronic, degenerative autoimmune dis-ease turned my life upside down. Before I became symptomatic, I had no idea that my life would change so dramatically. Forever. And yet, the changes in my life haven't been only about suffering, but also about peace, love, and spiritual awakening. My story started like this...

Out of the blue one day at work in the ER, my supervisor asked me if I was getting enough rest. She said my eyes didn't look well. I thought she was making idle conversation. But then I noticed tingling and numbness in my hands. When I reached out to touch people or objects, sharp shooting pains made me gasp and recoil. I spent a lot of time trying to stifle my tears.

I learned early in life ~ mistakenly, it turns out ~ that crying was a sign of weakness. And I believed that strong women did not cry. I didn't want to seem weak or vulnerable. I was secure, confident and happy. So when the pain threatened to drive me to my knees, I'd excuse myself to the ladies' room or back office, and then I'd let out the tears when no one was looking. On the way to work or alone at home, I would seek solace in my tears.

Eventually, I became afraid. The pain was getting downright inconvenient. It wasn't part of my life plan. One evening, I was preparing for an important dance recital at Atiyah Performing Arts School, where I taught voice techniques, worked as stage and production manager for shows, and was enrolled in a tap dance class.

I've always felt the pull of the irresistible energy I felt in the spotlight. So that night, I pushed away my pain. Instead, I asked a nurse at work to wrap both arms with some bright purple ace bandages that matched my outfit. And I went on with the show. I hurt like hell, but I was cute, and that's what counted for me then. It says a lot about what I valued at that time in my life.

Like so many of us that feel panicky when chronic pain begins to infringe on our lives, I began to hunt for anyone who could help me. A chiropractor first diagnosed me with Carpal Tunnel Syndrome in June 1995. I began to have regular chiropractic treatments where a machine injected electrical impulses through the nerves in my arms to relieve the pain. While it seemed to help at first, I began to notice that something new was happening. My hands, knees, feet and elbows were swollen and very painful every day. I underwent a series of grueling tests that ruled out the Carpal Tunnel Syndrome diagnosis, but nothing alleviated the pain.

I confided in no one but a single coworker, Snow, who felt safe to me. I was so afraid that people who knew me well would view me as weak and vulnerable if they knew about my strange symptoms. If I was caught crying, I was sure it would destroy the reputation I'd taken so long to build of a secure, confident, happy individual. I couldn't reconcile this new experience of myself with who I had been.

With each day that passed, something new seemed to malfunction in my body. My body felt locked in hell. I flip-flopped between hope and despair until at the end of that summer, in August 1995, my family practitioner told me I had Lupus, an incurable autoimmune dis-ease. According to the doctor, the results of the blood tests confirmed it.

I had been hoping he'd prescribe an antibiotic to clear up an inconvenient infection. Instead, I faced a Lupus diagnosis just an hour before my voice-over booking in Towson, Maryland. I left his office in a wild stupor with tears streaming down my face. The unexpected news at my doctor's office made me embarrassingly late for my booking, and I cried the entire 90-minute drive there. The longer I drove, the more desperate I became for some comforting words from someone who cared.

Impulsively, I phoned Kenney, the man I once considered the love of my life. I soaked the phone with tears and emotion, but didn't feel the empathy, assurance, and love I was seeking. In fact, it seemed that he'd moved on with his life and my pain would not be part of it. I felt rejected, embarrassed, and alone. I turned up the volume on the car stereo to drown my pain. I arrived at my booking in no mood to sound radiant on the radio.

But as it turned out, God sent an angel to the studio that day. I was compelled to tell my story and share my agony with this complete stranger. To my surprise, she said a beautiful and loving prayer for me before I entered the recording studio. It helped me summon the strength I couldn't muster on that life-changing day. I felt God's presence then and have continued to feel it every day since. She was the first of the many angels that have nurtured me on my journey towards healing.

When my family doctor told me I had Lupus that day, I told him with great conviction that "I might have it, but I won't keep it!" It wasn't until the following January, a full five months later, that I received an accurate and definitive diagnosis of Scleroderma. In the interim, I painfully shuffled into a rheumatologist's office every week. She was happy to write prescriptions for pain pills that didn't work, although she couldn't diagnose my dis-ease.

It wasn't until I described my agony during a routine visit to my OB-GYN that I finally received help. He was appalled that the doctor had whisked me in and out of her office weekly without a diagnosis for so many months. He worried about the possible progression of the dis-ease, particularly to my kidneys.

Chapter Two
On Seeing Doctors

"Our lives are limited or lifted by what we believe."

~ President Bill Clinton

After seeing many doctors, I've learned about the importance of being my own best advocate for my health. I am assertive with questions and concerns now. A typical doctor or specialist sees dozens of patients every day. Did you know that most clinicians can more easily recall the symptoms or diagnoses of the patients they saw that day than the color of their hair or eyes? For a doctor, each patient represents fifteen to forty minutes out of their day. But as patients, it is we who must leave with our pain and unanswered questions.

With the financial pressure from HMOs and insurers for doctors to see more patients, it's critical to take an active role in your own care. If you need to see a doctor, make a list of questions ahead of time and ask the receptionist to schedule enough time to address them. Keep a copy of your medical records and bring them with you to appointments with new health providers to ensure they have accurate information. Ask them to take time to review them carefully or send them prior to your appointment with this request. Would you believe that my original medical file said I was a 38 year old white woman with foster children taking oral contraceptives? When in fact, I was a 41 year old celibate childless black woman with no need or desire for birth control pills! Check your medical records. If you feel rushed through an appointment, say so. If you disagree with a treatment approach, express your concerns and ask for other options. Never hesitate to get a second opinion or appeal your health insurer's coverage decision. When you leave a doctor's office, ask yourself if you felt you were treated as a human being rather than a medical file. If not, find a new doctor or specialist. Your life counts!

Contrary to popular belief, many doctors do, however, care about their patients despite the current state of health care. When a rheumatologist at George Washington University Hospital, Washington, D.C., first diagnosed me, he was visibly upset about the dangerous stage to which my dis-ease had progressed. By then, I could no longer hide my emotional or physical pain and shared the news with my family. He graciously welcomed my mother into our consultation.

I was so relieved to finally learn what was wrong with me that the grim prognosis ~ just five years to live ~ did not even register then. But I did begin to feel more alone when I initially shared my news. I wasn't in a love relationship and my friends seem to be less available and stopped calling completely.

I think this is one of the most difficult parts of a chronic illness. It's easy to rally around someone with an acute illness, but what happens when it's chronic? While I continued on my marathon to survive, others drifted back to their own lives. They didn't know what to say or do. It's hard to be around someone who's sick. I wasn't much fun to be with. Spending time with someone who has a chronic illness can also force friends and family to contemplate their own mortality. While loving someone who is sick can be a growthful and heart-opening experience, many will not choose this path. In the end, people often find it's much easier to just stay away and be busy in their own lives.

Since I became ill, I have a better appreciation for those in pain. I no longer see them as "lesser than" because they can't walk, or catch their breath, or feel depressed. Sometimes just sitting next to someone with love and quiet is the best gift of all.

Chapter Three
Choosing Health

"He who conceals his dis-ease
cannot expect to be healed."

~ African Proverb

Despite my lack of emotional and physical support, I trudged on. Without the use of my hands or someone to help me, I struggled with daily functions. I couldn't buy essentials from the store because I was too tired and it was too painful to carry them. Circles around my eyes became darker and larger. Pain invaded every inch of my body. With swollen, hard, discolored skin, I cried whenever I attempted to bathe, comb my hair, or get out of bed. Routine blood tests were particularly painful because of my hardening skin and thinning veins. Ouch!

Perhaps one of the most devastating aspects of Scleroderma for victims is its disfiguring effect on facial skin. It masks its victims with a devilish rat-like look by pointing the nose while shrinking the skin around the mouth and making the teeth protrude. Most people with Scleroderma can recognize others with it because they share these features regardless of race or ethnicity. The emotional pain of seeing my own face was devastating. It was so hard to look at myself and see this other person as a reflection. I mourned the loss of the person I used to be and kept forcing my body to do the things that I used to do until the shock of the pain brought me back to reality. A walk to the mailbox was a major event for me.

The diagnosing rheumatologist recommended that I begin a course of Prednisone and D-penicillamine therapy to retard the progression of Scleroderma, a mysterious dis-ease with no known cause and no known cure.

He offered to treat me and also refer me for inclusion in clinical studies at Johns Hopkins in Baltimore. It was a lot to digest.

I was particularly concerned about the steroid medication Prednisone, that he'd recommended because I'd had a very unpleasant 14-day experience with it a decade earlier where it made me very sick with weight gain, a "moon face," and mood swings. Did I really need more misery?

I pondered my decision for a week and in the end elected not to take either medication based on my intuition that they would not be good for me. Ironically, since my decision in 1996, rheumatologists no longer prescribe high doses of steroids or D-Penicillamine for Scleroderma patients as they have since learned that they have the rare potential to induce severe high blood pressure and kidney failure in some Scleroderma patients.[3]

Another factor in my decision to skip the steroids was reconnecting with our family's long-time naturopathic physician, Dr. Gerald Douglass.[4] He had treated me successfully in my twenties for other less life-threatening health issues. While my mother was concerned about my decision to treat such a serious illness against the advice of a traditional medical specialist, she nonetheless, helped me track down Dr. Douglass. Serendipitously, his office turned out to be just a few blocks from where I was living at the time. He agreed with me that there were safer alternatives to steroids. I plunged into the world of alternative health care with diet changes, herbs, and vitamin supplements. Dr. Douglass told me that nutrition-packed sweet potatoes and yams are natural steroids, so I ate as many as I could. I started drinking fresh okra juice and using a product call Blue Green Algae.

Over the years, I tried many products and I learned that there is no magic bullet for healing. I tried some things that did more harm than good and others that were almost magical in their healing powers. I urge all who are sick and in pain to explore their own path to healing. Your experience will no doubt be unique and different from mine. Be open to both traditional and alternative healing modalities. Weigh side effects and benefits and trust your own inner

---

[3] Letter from Joseph P. Laukaitis, MD, August 3, 2000.

wisdom in making decisions. Be aware of your experience with different medications, supplements and strategies. Keep what works and toss out what doesn't. Seek out health practitioners ~ both traditional doctors and alternative care practitioners who have interest and knowledge about ways to integrate east and west healing modalities.

Since herbs are not regulated by the Food and Drug Administration (FDA), it is also important to have a healthy respect for mixing and matching these with pharmaceuticals. In fact, many pharmaceutical drugs are prepared from so-called "natural" herbs. Herbs may be more powerful than in their pharmaceutical forms so choose a knowledgeable herbalist and pharmacist if you choose to experiment in this realm. Be wary also of natural practitioners who don't ask for a list of medications you may be taking. Fortunately, traditional doctors are increasingly expanding their expertise into new therapies that were formerly belittled because of increasing consumer interest in them. Likewise, more holistic practitioners are becoming more informed about the effects of medications their patients may be taking.

It is my great hope that one day, patients can easily find medical care where we may take advantage of the full compliment of therapies without having to weigh the prejudices of traditional doctors against those of holistic practitioners.

---

[4] Naturopathic doctors are often considered as the general practitioners of the alternative health care world. They are trained in the general modalities of herbal medicine, acupuncture, clinical nutrition, dietary supplements, homeopathy, hydrotherapy, bodywork, and lifestyle counseling.

Chapter Four
Into Healing

"I release the need to have to wait for that which belongs to me."

~ Sheyla Shaw, personal friend

Healing often follows a circuitous route and proceeds more slowly than we would like. At times, death sounded more attractive to me than more medical treatments that would allegedly halt the progression of the dis-ease. I had many difficult days as I embarked on my new regimen. However, I also began to sense some subtle positive changes and feel hope on the horizon. My energy began to return. The hard snake like patches of skin on my face began to soften thanks to Mary Kay's night emollient creme. Symptoms began to wane and I noticed that I could walk without a cane again. It took less time to rise from bed in the morning and the pain that shot through my arms and legs lessened. I could move around more easily. My friend Rita and I discovered Dermablend, a cover-up cosmetic for my face, often used by burn victims. Most importantly, my determination to triumph over my death sentence began to grow.

As I delved into natural therapies, I also went on a reading jag. I began by reading all available medical literature on Scleroderma, and then moved on to practical life style information that I could incorporate into my life. I also learned about the mind-body-spirit connection from many sources.

During this period, I learned about the divine thread that connects everything in the universe. The mind, body and spirit connection is a reflection of that universal force. For homeostasis or total health to occur, there must be a balance of the three, just as an equilateral triangle has three sides that keep it in balance. Imagine yourself as the triangle, with a mental, physical and spiritual side. When your mental side is unbalanced, your physical and spiritual side will also be in decline. You the triangle, cannot be whole without all sides working equally towards balance. Health results from equilibrium.

I also learned about wisdom handed down from ancient civilizations. Everything in the universe is and has always been connected. The ancients taught that if one's spirit was not nurtured, then soon the body and mind would become imbalanced. Illness or death would soon follow.

I studied the ancient Ayurvedic traditions from India espoused by Deepak Chopra and Dr. David Simon; Feng Shui, the ancient art of Chinese placement; and many other texts from other civilizations and cultures.[5] But the message was always the same. Healing needed to take place in my mind, body, and spirit. I even pondered Louise Hay's thoughts on Scleroderma in her book *You Can Heal Your Life*. She offered emotionospiritual reasons for why
people contract certain dis-eases. In the case of Scleroderma, she believes people with this dis-ease are afraid to trust life, themselves, and God. I was skeptical... until I began my own inner spiritual journey and self-examination

---

[5] Ayurveda is a traditional healing system that originated in India. It utilizes natural means of dis-ease prevention including herbs, oils, minerals, heat massage, yoga, meditation, elimination therapy and counseling according to three body types (vata, pita and kapha). No particular treatment is offered for any specific symptom. Ayuvedic practitioners evaluate each client individually before offering treatments from a wide range of techniques including diet, herbal remedies, exercise, spiritual practices, and various healing modalities to bring a person into balance. In the Ayurvedic tradition, for example, a person with a heart problem would need to nourish her emotional heart as well as physical heart to achieve healing.

Chapter Five
My 40th Birthday

"Here is a test to find out whether your mission in life is complete.
If you are alive, it isn't."

~ Richard Bach

One of the first changes I made was a decision to celebrate my life. I did this in a big way on my fortieth birthday. Since I didn't know if it would be my last, I decided to indulge my dream of a very special celebration. As a July baby, my mid-summer birthday had always been a disappointment growing up. Family and friends seemed to be scattered and busy then, although my mother always made an effort to round up whomever she could to celebrate with me.

This party was different. Themed "A Rainbow Celebration of Life, "I sent out whimsical invitations that resembled theater tickets and offered to treat the first 100 friends who responded to a sumptuous, formal buffet dinner in the Crystal Room at the Washington Navy Yard in my hometown, Washington, D.C. I set up a special voice mailbox for responses, for my own amusement. And within 72 hours, I was well over my quota. My aunt suggested that maybe people responded quickly because of my free offer. I just laughed in amusement, knowing she was right. In the end, they were all there to celebrate me with me ~ friends from coast to coast ~ on a magical evening that made my birthday celebration dream come true. I reserved two limousines so my family and I could arrive in style. We ate. We danced, and I felt like a celebrity, even though I was exhausted by the close of the evening.

I think my fortieth birthday celebration was symbolic of becoming a more authentic person who began to ask for what she needed. Prior to the party, few of my friends knew I was sick or what I had been through, as I was so determined to hide it. In fact, there is an African proverb that says, "He who conceals his dis-ease cannot expect to be healed. "I learned this to be so very true the first few months out of the closet, living with Scleroderma. I was buoyed by a new surge of help and support.

On that special evening, I gave a speech that revealed my struggle with Scleroderma and expressed my gratitude for all those who were there to share my special day. As I tearfully chopped through the end of my speech, I cued the disc jockey to play Nancy Wilson's song, "Lady With A Song." Tears flowed freely, but I felt such a strong sense of love and support watching the long line of my friends and family approach me with tears in their eyes, love in their hearts, and outstretched arms. When my youngest sister Kim grabbed me and begged me not to leave her, we all cried about my dim prognosis. Even my father shed tears; he, who always said crying was a sign of weakness. Perhaps he felt a little weak from all the dancing? But as my friend Norman Bell likes to say: "The more you cry, the less you pee!"

Chapter Six
My Roots

"A squirrel ain't nothing
but a rat with a fuzzy tail."

~ Baxter "Rugged" Yarborough,
my daddy

The more I read about the mind-body-spirit connection, the more I began to wonder about my own attitudes and belief systems. Could my Scleroderma represent a physical manifestation of much more that need to be healed in me?

My fortieth birthday celebration was a catalyst for so many changes in my life as I worked to heal my body, mind, and spirit. Over time I became committed to rigorously self-examining my motives and my past, to learn how to act in ways that affirmed self-love and goodness. But before I could make these changes, I needed to become more aware of old patterns, which forced me to revisit old hurts, and old assumptions about myself and my life.

Since our childhood experiences mark us greatly, I decided to revisit my growing up years. As "the knee baby," in my family, I was as tall as my mother's knee when my baby sister Kim ~ the fifth child ~ was born. I consider my family "lovingly dysfunctional." Through the thread of my father's alcoholism and verbal and emotional abuse, love was the seam that held us together then and keeps us together today. Despite the many talents and gifts I developed, I also accumulated a lot of toxic waste in my life that I had held on to fiercely. I finally succumbed to the weight of it when Scleroderma forced the issue. Many experiences in school, at home, at work, and in love relationships reinforced my low self-esteem. I didn't know how to love myself. But Scleroderma taught me, for the first time, to put my own needs first.

Growing up in the 1960's and 70's, I'd lived with the chaos and confusion of my father's (we affectionately called him Rugged), two distinct and opposite personalities. When he was drinking, he was a loud, abusive tyrant who would announce his entrance in our quiet home with one loud bang on the front door followed by a barrage of profanities. I would brace myself for a long night ahead of cursing, crying, and fighting between my parents. I promised myself that when I grew up, I would never get married. And to date, I have kept that promise.

On those sleepless nights, I wondered why God would punish my family in this way. Why couldn't we be like other families? Years later, I learned that we were like other families. Many of my peers grew up with the trauma of family alcoholism. They just didn't talk about it. Rugged, however, liked to display his blood alcohol levels in public, so we had no secrets from our shame.

But when Rugged wasn't drinking, he was quiet and unassuming. He'd sleep or watch TV and leave the spanking to my mother. As the daughter of a Baptist minister, she tended and herded her flock of children and kept them together no matter what. She made excuses and denied our experience of our father. In fact, I can still hear her words in my head when we complained about our father's treatment of us: "No matter what. He is still your daddy."

We had to respect him. While she believed he would reap what he had sown in the afterlife, I only saw us suffering in this life. His dis-ease affected each of us and we all had our own way of expressing our pain. My oldest sister, Gwen, broke out with a devastating skin rash. My brother, Ronald, spent time fantasizing about a new life where he would rescue us and we'd live happily ever after. Instead, he fell victim to the streets received a brief prison sentence and ended up working for the Department Of Corrections. My sister, Nancy, closed up emotionally. And Kim clung to my mother, whined, tattled on everybody, and ate Twinkies. I felt hatred and wished upon him the same pain he had inflicted on our family. I began to doubt God. How could He stand by and watch our family be torn apart? The wait for relief seemed endless and the pain inside me grew fiercer every day.

When Ronald was just a tender teen, he moved out, seeking refuge with a dysfunctional family a few blocks away. At the time, I felt abandoned when we needed his protection most. It wasn't until years later that I could let go of this hurt and understand that he was doing what he could to soothe his own inner pain. Meanwhile, at home, I got angry with my mother for not protecting us. She would not leave Rugged or ask him to leave to save our family and it devastated me.

Chapter Seven
Suppressing Feelings

"And the day came when the risk
it took to remain tight inside the bud
was more painful than the risk
it took to blossom."

~ Anais Nin, author

As a child, I learned to suppress my feelings to protect myself from the pain. I often pretended that the verbal and emotional abuse at home didn't bother me the way it did others. After Ronald moved out, I felt I should be the strong one, and put myself in charge of keeping our family together.

I learned to use laughter and comedy as an outlet instead of tears. I don't know if I was more tired of crying or afraid to cry altogether. I had deep feelings as a child and no one to share them with. Despite my large family, I often felt alone. It never occurred to me that my siblings might share some of my feelings. We didn't talk about them.

While I've always been intelligent, I lacked self-confidence and self-esteem that was deeply rooted in my growing up years. As a young child, I didn't understand why my teachers fawned over the light-skinned girls and pushed away those of us who were blessed with beautiful dark skin. But this sort of racism left a mark on me that I couldn't erase. Even though I graduated from high school on the honor roll, attended an acclaimed university on a full scholarship, graduating with a double major and honors, I still grew up believing I would never be Good Enough.

So I just listened to the radio, watched TV, and looked at myself in the mirror a lot, wondering who I was and why was I put on earth. I remember spending hours peering at my reflection, and asking, "Who am I?" over and over again without ever being able to articulate a response that described and satisfied me. I'd pull myself into an abyss of confusion, until I gave up in frustration and tears.

I could only describe myself in relation to others. I didn't know how to capture my pure essence, my soul, and my real self. Now I believe my spiritual self was beckoning me to dig deeper inside myself. The mirror was really just a symbol of the self-reflection that I needed to do. It symbolized the difficulty I had then of seeing the light inside myself through my own eyes, the windows to my soul.

Later in life, I used these mirror-watching sessions in a more formal way to heal myself. I would stand consciously in front of the mirror, look closely into my own eyes and tell myself out loud about the things I loved about myself and the things I wanted to change. I cried. I laughed. I learned to take responsibility for the bad and the good, cleansing myself from all the negativity I'd carried around inside. It was another powerful tool that I used to facilitate my Scleroderma healing process spiritually, emotionally and physically.

My childhood friendships also sustained me. I first met Ntianu (aka Deborah Burke) in fourth grade when she was new to Garfield Elementary. I always reached out to newcomers and she responded. We've been close ever since, even though our lives have taken us on different paths to different places. From elementary to high school, Ntianu and I spent a lot of time with our close friends Denise, Jackie, Carolyn, and Gail. I am proud to have been a part of their lives during those formative years.

My love of music and performing started early in life during the many hours I spent listening to the radio and watching television. It provided an excellent diversion from my confusing home life. I idolized The Supremes, Honey West, Lois Lane, Gladys Knight, and Annette Funicello from the Mickey Mouse Club. I dreamed of becoming a famous star like Diana Ross. I was a great imitator of these childhood idols and could mimic almost any voice I heard on a sixties' TV show. I did an especially good impression of Granny's wrenching whine and Miss Jane's stiff lipped monotone from the Beverly Hillbillies' series!

Despite the hidden racism in Washington, D,C. classrooms in the 1950's and 60's, and a host of other problems, the public school system did respect and revere the arts, affording me many opportunities to fuel my passion for performing. Even in my elementary school years, I always performed in a glee club, choir, or chorus. Sometimes the simplest events shape our lives. I can still remember my excitement at age eight upon reading in the play "The Littlest Angel" at Garfield Elementary School in southeast Washington, DC. I credit that experience with prompting my interest in reading professionally (i.e. voice-overs) in later years.

I enjoyed entertaining anyone who would listen long enough. My siblings and I made daily calls to the on-air personalities of WOL-AM, the number one Black radio station at the time. Back then, the disc jockey personalities loved to entertain and get to know their audiences. We took maximum advantage of their willingness with our daily song requests, contest entries, or calls to chat. My sister Nancy was the instigator, with her frequent requests for Smokey Robinson songs. I know we must've been annoying, but despite that, we got well-acquainted with Bobby Bennett, the top jock during that time.

Bobby would eventually come to know the entire family and be instrumental in helping land my first job in radio at WOL-AM. Our relationship has now lasted over three decades; we consider him our adopted brother. He helped to shape my career in the broadcast industry. I will always be grateful for all that I learned from him and his partner, the talented voice artist, Jack Daniels (an assumed name for his radio persona).

When I turned fourteen, I decided I wanted to become the first female disc jockey. Since I also liked the idea of owning a brand new sports car, I was pleased to learn a DJ's salary could afford to foot the bill. I refined my life plan over the next few years and decided I'd go to college, get a communications degree, and become America's first black female radio announcer. They made more money.

Unfortunately, some older women took the job right out from under my aspiring young feet! I was proud to hear the eloquent voices of Robyn Holden on WHUR-FM, J. Marie Morris on WOL-AM and Candy Shannon on WKYS-FM. It didn't matter anymore for me to be the first female African American DJ. Instead, I wanted to be one of the best, by studying and emulating the talented voices of these phenomenal women over the airwaves.

Although I loved music, the spoken word also had a power that drew me into a world of wonder and amazement. So I started to dream that one day I would sound as good as my idols did. That day came many years later in 1989 when I began my career as a professional voice-over artist.

Chapter Eight
Ministry and Music

"Life is a song, sing it!"

~ Mother Teresa

I was raised a Baptist, where I learned about God. But it wasn't until I was older and our family began to worship at a more contemporary church that I first felt God. At Union Temple Baptist Church (UTBC), worshipers shouted, swayed, and sung their praise to the Lord. Instead of suppressing all my feelings as at home, I found a welcoming place where I could let out all the feelings I had. There was Spirit in the music. It uplifted me and helped me cope with my home life. I was in awe of the energy and music of the star divas in the young adult choir, directed by Richard Smallwood, which had already recorded one album.

Eventually I joined the choir and recorded on its second album. I was living my dream to sing professionally at last! Between my excitement over the singing and my admiration for the articulate, charismatic young minister, I forgot to join the church for nearly two years. It's also where I began my lifelong fantasy of the ideal man. I dreamed of a husband who would love me the way this young pastor did his fiancée. He called her his "black diamond." And, she is in fact a jewel... one who stayed close to my family and I over the years. Now we call her "Sister Pastor," as she's now a reverend too. Unfortunately, this romantic fantasy didn't serve me very well as I continued my search for my soulmate in adulthood.

My Good Enough thoughts dogged me though, even after I joined the church and traveled extensively with the choir, which was increasingly booked on weekends and during the week. I longed for a solo part and prayed that one day Richard would notice I had a nice voice and give me a coveted solo, but it didn't happen. My low self-esteem sunk lower. I wanted to be a diva ~ and quick. After all I was planning to be the next Diana Ross and I had no time to waste.

But I kept on singing for the Lord and learned that singing in the background offered its own rewards. I learned a lot about the importance of harmony in music, perhaps planting a small seed of how to find the right tone and balance in my adult life. The Young Adult Choir of Union Temple Baptist Church was a trailblazer in message music ~ music inspired by God ~ in the seventies and eighties. Our demanding travel schedule afforded lots of opportunity to meet interesting people and bless those who heard our music. The choir was my social life then, so naturally I was always searching for that special man who would catch my eye and win my heart at UTBC.

Chapter Nine
Higher Education

"The world you desire can be won. It exists, it's real,it is possible, it's yours."

~ Ayn Rand, author

I graduated from Anacostia Senior High School in southeast Washington, D.C. in 1974. Despite the fact that I had enough credits to graduate after eleventh grade, I had very little college counseling on how to apply for grants and scholarships. Looking back now, I wonder why. Was it because I wasn't an honor roll student the full three years or was it because of my skin color?

To fulfill graduation requirements, I participated as a senior in a work-study program. The D.C. Air National Guard wasn't a good fit for me, so I ended up working afternoons in the pediatric emergency room at the city hospital instead. At eighteen, I found the job interesting but wondered about the jealousy and petty bickering among co-workers that lurked within those walls of healing. It comforted me to spend breaks with my old friends Deborah and Denise who worked in other hospital departments since it was our first separation since elementary school. I reaffirmed my commitment to go on to college, get a degree in broadcasting, become a radio announcer and buy myself a sports car.

Four years later, in 1978, I received my B.A. in both Sociology and Communications from The American University in Washington, DC. I was a Frederick Douglas Scholar on full scholarship to one of the most prestigious schools in the country, thanks to Tony Brown,

Dean of the School of Communications at Howard University.

I had applied to Howard University upon graduating high school, but was denied admission to the School of Communications because my SAT scores weren't Good Enough. Some guidance counseling on academic work, grants and scholarships during my years at Anacostia High would have been invaluable in helping me navigate my path towards Howard, the college I had my heart set on attending, but it didn't happen.

God has a way of fixing things though. When my mother and I showed up one hot summer day at the Dean's office at Howard University to express our anger and disappointment about the rejection letter, Tony Brown, a complete stranger to me then, listened carefully and excused himself to make a phone call. When he returned he offered a contact and phone number at The American University (AU). There I received a scholarship for tuition and room and board on campus. In the end, AU was the right place for me. Attending a multicultural school exposed me to a wider world and more diverse learning than my experience growing up in a black community could have ever done.

While at AU, I founded the AU Gospel Choir in the spring of 1976. This special choir is now well-recognized, frequently featured at important school functions and appears on local television shows. I am proud that I helped them get their start.

I had started singing in weddings while in college with my good friend and kindred spirit Raymond. Eventually, after giving away my talents for free, I started a wedding music service with Raymond, a talented writer, musician and vocalist. Much like myself, Raymond was multi-talented. He had traveled the world touring with various artists and would pull me in on musical theater and recording projects whenever possible.

Raymond and I share similar, tastes, interests, and sun signs... we're both Leos! We also share challenges with self-esteem. While

I love him like a brother, I knew then that he too had so much more to offer the world than he was giving. Why? Because I was doing the same thing! We were both stuck in a cycle of maybe not being Good Enough and couldn't find a path out.

Raymond was a gifted writer and penned the love ballad, "With You," sung by Tony Terry. That song put him on the map towards a rewarding writing career. Former Washington, D.C. Mayor Marion Barry even commissioned him to compose a song for his second wedding. But despite these phenomenal successes, I knew he had so much more inside of him. But there was something holding him back. That something was himself. The doubts and the fears that haunted me, clutched at him too.

We would often discuss our life struggles and puzzle about the way we managed to sabotage our own best efforts. I remember one occasion when we were introduced to the famous jazz vocalist Nancy Wilson. She recognized Raymond from Tony Terry's song, told us she was looking for love songs to record on her upcoming album Love, Nancy, and asked us to submit some music for her consideration. What a thrill! I had just finished a series of love song lyrics for Raymond to put to music that would be perfect. We left that night full of enthusiasm and imagining Nancy singing our songs on her album. But time passed. So did the deadline. And before we knew it, the album had been released without a single attempt to send her our songs.

Before Scleroderma, I thought I had a lifetime to build my career in music. I let so many chances slip by. I didn't know then that my lungs would be permanently scarred at age 40, leaving me unable to sing again. You never know what life will bring. Now I try to embrace life more fully, seizing each moment. As for Sir Raymond, he is now the proud owner of a Grammy Award. He won it for his inspired production of the CD Experience, by Grammy-award winning gospel artist Yolanda Adams.

Chapter Ten
The Men in My Life

"Only illusion can collapse.
Our true inner self remains."

~ David Richo, psychotherapist

Many people come in and out of your space during our lives. Some encounters are temporary, some are permanent some are stagnant. But all come for a reason. People came into my life to teach me valuable lessons. And it wasn't always the nice people I learned from. In fact, I believe my most important lessons came from those people that I thought hurt me in some way. This was usually, but not always, a man with whom I was involved.

Over the years I've been involved with men who could neither appreciate nor respect and love me the way I felt I deserved. Like many women, I lacked self-confidence and would do and accept almost anything just to have a man in my life. Like many women, the ones that I wanted didn't want me, but the ones I didn't want did. In reality, men were often in my life when it was convenient for them. It took gallons of tears and years of fears for me to see that my happiness and self-worth were not measured by the man I let share my bed.

I was smart enough to pass on the men I knew were married, in a relationship, addicted to cigarettes or alcohol or non-spiritual. On the other hand, when there was a man that I wanted, I would not rest until I had him.

Willie and I met in sociology class at American University. He was handsome, charismatic, intelligent, and articulate. He was single and spiritual. Best of all, I learned that he loved gospel, R&B and jazz. He went to church and believed in God. In fact, he wanted to be a minister. Remember how I'd always wanted to marry a minister? I was smitten.

However, he was a social butterfly. I learned that he had other love interests. And yet I continued to see him without requiring a commitment from him, because I believed I wasn't Good Enough to ask for more. We connected musically though, too, and eventually formed a gospel singing group on campus as a trio of vocalists with a pianist to accompany us during performances at the Kay Spiritual Life Center on campus. We were good together in many ways and I was sure he was the man I'd been waiting for.

But despite my best efforts to convince him we were soulmates, Willie and I weren't meant to be. He struggled during those years in defining a future for himself… torn between his desire to be a jazz singer and to do God's will. I was very needy in those days and he was very popular with the ladies. I know now we weren't the right match romantically.

Willie went on to seminary school, earned his Masters of Theological Studies and was recently voted one of the top five motivational speakers worldwide by Toastmasters for his unique blend of "inspirtainment." In fact, he's currently the feature artist on ABC Rejoice Radio Network's nationally syndicated radio show "The Willie Jolley Motivational Minute."

I'm pleased that Willie has found a way to inspire others with his spiritual message by joining his desire to sing and serve the Lord with his charisma and gifts as an inspirational professional speaker. Willie continues to be a close friend and blessing to me throughout the years, especially since my diagnosis with Scleroderma. He's never been too busy to say a prayer for me, to call or drop me a line. In fact, he often shares my story with his audiences in seminar appearances and radio interviews. I told him once that I'd rather have a lifelong friend than a part-time lover. So you see, he's been very committed to me ~ through some of the darkest days of my life ~ just not in the way I expected. When we split in college, however, I was sure I couldn't go on without him. I was wrong again.

Chapter Eleven
A Rugged Recovery

"So stick to the fight when you're hardest hit. It's when things go wrong that you must not quit."

~ Unknown

While I was off at college, my father, of course, continued to drink... a practice he'd begun half a lifetime ago to deaden the pain of racial injustices he'd suffered growing up in the south and later, the post-traumatic stress disorder (PTSD) he acquired during his military service in World War II. When I got the call that he'd been hospitalized for Pancreatitis with surgery scheduled, I thought back to my mother's often repeated words about how he'd someday reap what he sowed. I remembered my childhood wish that he'd someday feel all the pain that he'd caused my family and me.

But when I witnessed all his pain while visiting him in his hospital room at the local VA Hospital, I could only see him as a soul who needed some healing from the Master Physician, Mother/Father God. Despite the hatred I felt towards him in my childhood, I felt sorry for him in that moment. It was then that I stopped tolerating my father and began to forgive him and love him. As a young adult, I was able to better understand his struggles and personal demons.

Rugged eventually sought help for and successfully recovered from his alcoholism, integrating those two distinct personalities into a single wonderful individual. Rugged used to say, "I'm not an alcoholic. I'm a drunk... because alcoholics have to go to those damn meetings!" I began then a new and very rewarding relationship with my dad and new friend. I also experienced the joy of watching my parents grow closer with love and affection.

During summers off from school, I never thought to pursue a job in broadcasting, my field of interest. Duh! I went back where it was safe... to that same city hospital, DC General (aka DC Germ). In fact, whenever I needed work over the next nine years, I could always count on it being there. I worked in medical records, on the surgery ward, OB-GYN, Pediatrics, ER, Admitting and Ambulatory Surgery. It was easy. Safe. Familiar. But in later years, it also proved to be stifling.

Long before the popular television show ER aired on TV, I'd spent many years absorbing the stories and pain from this inner city hospital. Deaths by gunshot wounds. Stabbings. Assaults with baseball bats and ice picks. Sick criminals. I saw it all. It was a wrenching experience, so as usual, I used humor to mask my pain. Smoking in public places was legal then, so even though I didn't smoke, my hair and clothes reeked of it and I developed a smoker's cough.

The disregard for hygiene in the public and employee restrooms began to take its toll on me the day I discovered human feces smeared throughout each of the bathroom walls and stalls. I earned the name "The Bag Lady" for showing up with my own bucket of ammonia and cleaning supplies for my work area, and began showering and washing my clothes after work each day. The emotional baggage I was carrying, however, weighed much more than the cleaning supplies because it sucked away my life force. Now I wonder why I stayed in such a place for so long instead of following my dreams. A sort of self-punishment for not being Good Enough I suppose.

After graduating from AU, I moped around for a year wondering why the big broadcasting stations weren't breaking down my door with employment offers. Didn't they know how good I was? I had co-hosted "Sacred Sounds," the on-campus gospel radio show. I was the founder of The AU Gospel Choir. I was a member of one of the country's hottest gospel choirs, the Union Temple Baptist Church Young Adult Choir, directed by the renowned artist Richard Smallwood. Heck... I was a personal friend of Bobby Bennett at WOL radio! But I was unemployed, depressed, and as broke as a church mouse.

Job leads in radio were slim. And it always felt like there was an invisible brick wall in front of me that kept me from reaching my potential. I even applied with the government agencies, Voice of America, and the U.S. Information Agency. The programming was dull, but the pay was excellent. I was well qualified for jobs I applied for in broadcasting. I was sure one audition would pan out, but I received yet another rejection letter. This was not very good for my already bruised ego. It felt like another confirmation that I was just Not Good Enough.

It took me awhile to get over my sense of rejection, but after a grueling long year, I finally landed a job as music research director at my favorite radio station WOL-AM and planned to work up to becoming an announcer.

But just as things were finally looking up, rumors circulated about the station's legal troubles and it was sold to new owners. I interviewed for an on-air position at a new gospel radio station, WYCB-AM, slated to begin broadcasting late that summer.

At the interview, I prattled on about the music I would play and was sure the job was in the bag. When I didn't get it, I became bitter... especially towards God, who seemed to be making life so difficult for me and wouldn't give me what I wanted and needed (like my sports car!). But as time passed, I learned that God hadn't said, "no," but just "not yet."

I moved to Charlotte, NC to live with my sister Nancy and her family and was hired as a public service director and weekend announcer on WGIV-AM radio. After working in Charlotte for four months, I was called back to DC to the new gospel station, WYCB-AM, in the nation's capitol. Program Director Vashti McKenzie (now the first female Bishop of the African Methodist Episcopal Church Worldwide) had heard my demo tape and hired me for the overnight shift.

I worked in radio for about five years. But I became disillusioned working at low budget AM gospel stations where employees stole money and crazy general managers made false accusations and fired DJs only to hire them back at a lower wage. After one such station, WUST closed due to financial problems, I went back to work at DC General until I could "do better."

Chapter Twelve
Health care Makes Me Sick

"Life is a challenge. Meet it."

~ Mother Teresa

Having worked in a hospital off and on through the years, however, I started to become more sensitive to the environment there. One of the first things I noticed was how little health care professionals washed their hands as they moved from one patient to the next. They were working with an inner city population with poor hygiene to begin with and all kinds of bodily fluids in the ER. They checked IDs and took signatures from patients with fresh blood on them. I watched health care workers use the restroom, treat patients, eat and share food without washing their hands. Eweh!!!!

This exists across hospitals in every state with the crush to work faster with less support and resources, despite strict regulations by governmental and hospital accreditation organizations about hygienic practices. Frankly, it appalled me. My parents had taught me about the art of thorough handwashing at an early age. It's a simple ritual I live by daily. It is hard for me to understand why so many people omit this from their daily practice, especially with so many dis-eases afloat. Although I do notice that the media doesn't help. In fact, television shows often portray people preparing meals without washing their hands!

It was also the beginning of a phobia surrounding germs and bathrooms that I'm still working on healing. Eventually, I began to take note of who washed and who didn't. I politely declined homemade dishes the non-hand washers brought into the breakroom to share with co-workers. I started to think about the doorknob at the hospital's entrance where all those ER cases entered. I pondered the implications of our sharing writing utensils and handling the same papers, but with different standards for hygiene.

I felt like I was spending a great deal of time in a cesspool of dirt, dis-ease and death. Sometimes the stench of a sick or poorly kept patient would be enough to make me want to vomit. But I had to pay my rent, so I continued to work at the hospital until 1989 when I decided to follow my dream and become a voice-over artist.

One day I got a call from a friend and former radio associate, Bob, who was working as an announcer then on WHUR-FM in Washington, DC. We were both interested in providing voice talent for commercials but neither of us had any idea how to go about actually getting clients outside of the radio stations. So when Bob invited me to attend a seminar with him in New York City on how to become voice-over talent, I was excited.

As soon as we opened our mouths to tape mock auditions in front of the class, it was clear to Susan Berkley, our instructor, that we were seasoned professionals. I felt that finally I'd found my niche... something I enjoyed and I was Good Enough to do successfully.

The seminar, of course, finished on a high note, assuring us that with our talent and the proper marketing, we could be making six figure incomes in no time. "So when do I start?" I thought, with dollar signs in my eyes.

Although I was still working at the hospital, I was ready to make a move into my creative destiny, so I used my good credit to arrange one of those 15-minute approval loans from my bank for $5,000 to finance a demo tape, resume and headshot.

I went back to New York, recorded my demo tape and sent out over 100 tapes with headshot to the casting world. Within six months, I landed my first job for PEPCO, (the Potomac Electric Power Company) in a two-voice characterization commercial. I remember meeting the beautiful and talented broadcaster Angela Stribling there.

I was prepared to dislike Angela immensely because she seemed to have all that I wanted: beauty, brains, a big bank account, and major broadcasting contracts. My green-eyed monster reared its ugly head. But as we rehearsed, my jealousy turned to admiration. When I offered a dramatic confession of my ill feelings of her in the elevator as we left the studio, she met it with a hearty laugh, warm hug and later… a number of referrals that I appreciated greatly.

I went on to do voice-overs for nine years, making what I called "stupid money," (because it seemed so easy!), but eventually I got complacent. I ignored what I knew about the need to continually market myself since I had a steady clientele and it was easier to wait for the referrals to come in. While I had all the contacts, resources, and talent I needed to make an excellent income, I also allowed my insecurities about becoming Good Enough to detour me from success. Eventually, the jobs grew fewer and my bank account slimmer.

I decided to supplement my income and went back into hospital work. After free-lance jobs during the day, I'd work the evening shift in the emergency room at a small community hospital in Maryland. I was a full-time admitting officer, aka a clerk. Despite being a seasoned veteran working in hospitals since I was sixteen, this job was the most challenging for me. The job title did not quite cover all I did. We were overworked and underpaid. I was actually a telephone operator, customer service representative, financial counselor, patient escort, registrant, data entry clerk, interviewer, patient liaison, public relations representative, social worker, grief counselor, admitting and bed board coordinator, and discharge clerk with a too small staff.

The climate in an Emergency Room changes from minute to minute, much like working on the front lines in wartime. The dramas in the lobby, the curt and demanding attitudes of many physicians, and the waves of ER traumas made me hyper alert. Emotions ran high and I had to work hard to maintain my composure. This became a daily challenge that profoundly affected me as the negativity and emotion weaved its way into my psyche.

When patients needed to be heard, they spoke with me. When they wanted to complain about their treatment or diagnosis, they hunted me down. I made myself available to those in need. But usually, my kindness was taken for granted. I often felt drained from the emotional roller coaster I was on.

Looking back now, I see how I caused this myself by allowing myself to become too involved with patients. So many "regulars" would come looking for me because they knew that I would do whatever it took to get them what they wanted.

Over time, I learned that less than 25% of patients who came into the ER really needed emergency care. Most just needed some attention or emotional support. I remember when Mayor Marion Barry was blasted once by the media for stating that D.C. ambulances were being used as a taxicab service. He was telling nothing but the truth. I was there, on the front lines at the city hospital, and saw it every day.

Negligent mothers would call the ambulance instead of the pediatrician in the middle of the night because their child had vomited... 2 weeks prior this 2 week-long sudden emergency was often a ploy to round up her baby's daddy, who was spending too much time with his other baby's momma or hanging with his boys. Ambulance drivers seethed at these summons when real emergencies ~ like the toddler who died because her parents put PCP in her milk bottle to hide it from police ~ were waiting. Once, a patient came in to the ER for treatment and was unhappy with the wait. He walked two blocks and summoned an ambulance in an effort to be seen more quickly! How smart was that? And before you ask... no it didn't work!!!!

It is amazing to me now how I allowed myself to be sucked into the emergency room dramas at both hospitals where I worked. Perhaps I did so because it felt familiar. Once again, I was the caretaker who would smooth everything over, just as I had done as a child for my family. And yet, I was angry with myself. I was overqualified, underpaid and "settling" again, instead of mindfully building my future in broadcasting.

Chapter Thirteen
The Politics of Medicine

"One's disability has nothing to do with one's ability."

~ Theodore "Teddy" Pendergrass, R&B vocalist

As a health care worker on the front lines, I got an up close look at how medicine worked. My experiences at both hospitals reinforced my distrust of the system I had personally experienced.

During my days as a radio announcer, I once consulted a general practitioner for a sore throat and received an unnecessary breast exam and medication that made me sick. My sore throat wasn't diagnosed or aided by the medication.

I needed my voice to work so I continued to take the medication and show up for my midnight shift at the radio station. I threw up every morning at 5 am in the studio trash can for a week as my anger grew. I felt taken advantage of because I had been so trusting. Now I know how important it is to ask questions when a doctor prescribes a medication and to express concerns for any type of treatments that do not feel comfortable (i.e. a breast exam) or call back to report any side effects or request a new approach. I know that if I don't advocate for myself, no one will ~ especially not a busy doctor! But remember, you pay their salary. You have rights.

When I worked in hospital emergency rooms, the hospital kept a file on so-called "drug-seekers," who would present to get drugs for their addiction and then be turned away. I used to look at these individuals with disgust, until I realized their addiction was often a result of an initial addictive prescription that caused side effects that required more drugs. This "Band-Aid" approach to treating patients can eventually create a drug addict. I know now from experience. While a typical hospital spends much time ensuring that insurance information is accurate so it gets paid for the patient's visit, its caregivers spend precious little time referring addicts for counseling at a treatment facility. They're too busy handing out prescriptions!

I have found that the politics of medicine hinders the healing process for patients with dis-ease. Doctors are often members of "medical group practices" which then negotiate fees on their behalf in exchange for contracts with large insurance companies. The trend towards "managed care" has transferred the power base from doctors who used to make exorbitant salaries to insurance companies who now make tremendous profit instead.

Patients, employers, and actually, even doctors, are caught in the middle of a health care machine that has no mercy and can afford little care. Insurers provide powerful incentives for employers and patients to sign up with "health maintenance organizations" (HMOs) where patients can only see approved doctors. These doctors have agreed to reduce their fees to secure enough business. They see dozens of patients a day that are referred by the HMO, leaving them 15 to 40 minutes or so to write a prescription and move on to the next patient. Increasingly, many doctors are refusing to accept HMO patients because they don't like to practice this kind of factory approach to health care.

But isn't your health the most important thing in the world? I believe it's important to shop for doctors, even more thoroughly than you would for an attorney.[6] When your health is at stake, can you afford to blindly choose an HMO doctor name out of a book?

Increasingly, patients are enrolling in Preferred Provider Organization (PPO) or other similar insurance through their employers. While this allows you the freedom to see any doctor or specialist you deem necessary, it also comes with a heavy price tag. Deductibles can be astronomically higher than those through HMO programs. Hospitalization costs and the percentage you pay for routine visits will also tend to be much higher. Insurance companies like to keep patients in cost-controlled HMOs. You or your employer may not be able to afford a PPO program.

Only you can make the decision about what you can afford and the importance of choosing your own doctors. But what you can do is check up on the doctors and hospitals you choose to see. Recently, the U.S. government began to release "hospital report cards."[6] This consumer mechanism for measuring quality care is still being refined and so shouldn't be considered definitive proof of quality and safety, but it's certainly better than choosing a name out of a book.

The reality is, many dis-eases today are considered to have "no cure" by medical experts. If you suffer from such a dis-ease, you can at least insist on doctors who will take time to speak with you, treat you as a fellow human being, monitor your care, and return your calls when you have questions about new research you read about, new symptoms you are experiencing, or medication side effects.

On a positive note, scientific research is making significant strides. On the flip side, only research on new pharmaceuticals gets funded. Furthermore, only drugs with the greatest profit potential for large pharmaceutical companies are funded. Make no mistake: healthcare is big business. If you search for research papers or clinical data about the effects of certain herbs or alternative medicine, you will be disappointed.

Pharmaceutical companies will never pay for expensive clinical trials focusing on the efficacy of alternative therapies, especially since such therapies generally can't be patented. There is no financial incentive. And our government, although it now funds such projects through its National

---

[6] Check out hospital "report cards" before your next stay as an inpatient. Many websites offer free information and "ratings" of hospitals, physicians, and specialists according to procedures. One such website, www.healthgrades.com includes useful information on how to choose a doctor, hospital, acupuncturists, long-term care facility and more. You can even look up information on specific physicians in your area. Some states are also setting up similar websites for state-specific information. Be cautious when interpreting data though. (For instance, complications could be higher at one hospital than another if they specialize in seeing sicker or older patient populations.)

Institutes of Health (NIH), has been embarrassingly slow to fund and conduct government-sponsored clinical trials, though I believe that many citizens would support tax dollars used for such ground-breaking research.

Increasingly however, patients are gravitating to alternative therapies anyway. The millions of dollars that disenfranchised consumers pour into these therapies out of their own pockets, has made players in health care sit up and take notice. Many hospitals are adding massage, meditation, aromatherapy and other "new age" therapies to their care as they work to increase market share. As you try to make your way through the maze of difficult decisions without good data, I urge you to become informed and also use your intuition and experiment with what works for you.

The truth is, people are being cured every day from so-called incurable dis-eases by using "age-old" simple techniques that integrate mind/body/spirit modalities into healing. Are these concepts "new age?" Many of these concepts arise from times long past, when people lived off the land, and had no pharmacies to access for prescriptions. They relied on wise men and women who shared their knowledge of medicinal herbs and holistic practices to facilitate healing. Although their "medicine" was often sound and effective, history attests to many healers who were persecuted or murdered.

Many of the alternative therapies recommended today are simply those passed down through generations from our forefathers in different cultures and countries around the world. Simple cures like rock candy and rye for a cold… garlic to lower blood pressure… licorice root for a sore throat. They worked for our ancestors, so why not now? Let's be selective about the therapies we choose, taking advantage of modern scientific advances in treatment of dis-ease as well as age-old wisdom.

Chapter Fourteen
What's Love Got to Do with It?

"Love is a smoke made with the fume of sighs. Being purged, a fire sparkling in lovers' eyes... What is it else? A madness most discreet, a choking gall and a preserving sweet."

~ William Shakespeare

When I met Kenney, I was just 21. I first caught a glimpse of him during choir rehearsal one Saturday at UTBC. He looked so much like my old friend Richard, the choir director, that I wondered if Richard was taking up a new instrument.

I didn't know then that this would be the man who would win my heart and become the love of my life. I was still trying to hang on to the unrequited love of my college days, Willie. So while I was flattered, when he asked a mutual friend to introduce us, I wasn't interested. I made up excuses to avoid dates and didn't return his calls. I was cool to him and kept a force field around my heart to avoid being hurt again. I told myself that Kenney was too young, too light-skinned and too sensitive to be with me. My dark skin might not make me Good Enough.

Actually, his sensitivity, spirituality, and intellect were exactly what I needed. And his determination also matched mine when it came to love. He waited patiently and showed me what a man in love looked like. He wrote me poems and songs and was courteous. So, after nine months of watching him chase me, I opened my eyes to a bright new beginning and embraced the new love of my life.

Not only was he handsome, but we had similar hobbies and interests. It was a joy to be with him. While he was three years my junior, he was light years ahead of me spiritually. Actually he embodied all the qualities I most respected in a man. It took almost a year, but his persistence paid off. Finally, on Christmas Eve 1980, I gave in to this handsome young man. We became the best of friends, lovers, and co-workers. Kenney was a musician and a promotional photographer. I was a vocalist and radio personality. When our professional paths crossed, it was electrifying! We went on to have a wonderful five-year relationship. I was elated.

Kenney's family welcomed me with open arms. None of my other male friends had invited me to their parents' home or family gatherings. In contrast, Kenney's mom, Gwen, prepared a special meal on the occasion of our meeting.

"She doesn't like phony people," he cautioned me as we rode out into the rural suburbs of Upper Marlboro, Maryland that first evening. Once again, I worried I might not measure up. Black on black racism is still alive and well. Maybe she'd judge me on my skin color like my teachers had? What if she didn't want me dating her light skinned son?

His mother was beautiful and shared her son's deep, dark eyes and winning smile. I decided to just be me and hope for the best. Gwen greeted me warmly and made an incredible dinner of fried chicken wings, macaroni and cheese, string beans and homemade rolls. I ate three full plates without missing a beat! She laughed and offered more. I think when I left that day I even asked for a doggie bag for leftovers. Twenty-two years later, Gwen still likes to tell the story of our first meeting. She has loved me over the years as if I was one of her own children. I was Good Enough for her.

But my family wasn't so welcoming to Kenney. My mother didn't like him and this confused me at first. Now I know that in any relationship or family dynamic, upheaval happens when one person begins to act differently. In my family, I was the caretaker, the one who could be counted on when anyone needed anything. But as I began to get a life of my own, I wasn't as available and this made my mother extremely uncomfortable. She depended most upon me, among all my siblings.

My mother's dislike of Kenney was fueled by some hearsay information on how Kenney allegedly used women. She refused to get to know him for himself, although my father respected my choice. Trying to manage the relationship between Kenney and my mother became anguishing and emotionally draining. I felt stretched between the people I loved. I didn't know where my to pledge my allegiance!

Eventually, I chose to move out of my family home and into an English basement apartment on Capitol Hill with Kenney. That met with much Christian opposition from my mother. But I was 21 and ready to try "living in sin." It suited me well for awhile.

Kenney asked me to marry him repeatedly. Although I was in love with him, I was afraid of marriage. Afraid I might not be Good Enough as a wife. I hadn't grown up with any examples of loving, respectful marriages. The married women I knew dressed sloppily and acted old, tired and bored. The men grew big stomachs and complained about their wives. My own parents were a study in conflict. I rarely witnessed them being affectionate to each other and this affected the way I viewed relationships, intimacy, and marriage. I felt sure that if I married Kenney, we would end up miserable, like my parents seemed to be. It would ruin our epic love. When I was young, I promised myself I would never get married because I didn't want to be another divorce, alcoholism, or battery statistic.

While Kenney and I lived together, I became pregnant with his child. The relationship died a terrible death on his birthday, not long after I miscarried our beautiful daughter, whom we planned to name Keva. I didn't know how to mourn my personal loss openly so I did what I'd always done since childhood. I buried all the hurt, fear, and raw emotional pain deep inside. I carried the guilt of losing my child around with me for many years, with no idea of the impact this would have on the rest of my life.

Losing Kenney was one of the biggest regrets in my life. There were so many things working against the success of our relationship. It was so difficult to give of myself completely at the beginning. Then, when we finally caught on fire, my mother's rejection nagged at me. The miscarriage was the final straw.

I went on to have other relationships with men, but they never worked out either. Some of my choices were questionable to say the least, and certainly reflected my low self-esteem.

I met Sam in 1991. Although I was immediately attracted to him and wanted to explore possibilities of romance, our friendship was loosely platonic. And this was fine for him... without commitments or emotional ties. I would call on him when I wanted male companionship and intimacy that he did not provide. He called on me when he was returning my phone calls.

He often showed me his dark side but I refused to see that he was toxic, obsessive-compulsive, manic-depressive and dangerous because he once involved me in a life-threatening situation. He used my apartment to hide out from his world of chaos and confusion, revenge and espionage. All I wanted to do was slide my way into his heart by showing him that I was a loyal friend and an excellent choice for a life partner. All he wanted was the safe haven that I lovingly provided. I allowed him to dishonor me and my constitution as well as endanger my life. But when it was his turn to help me during my life-threatening health crisis, he left me without a trace.

Sam was one of the few people who I allowed to see me when I was very sick. One day, he saw my naked and deformed face and disappeared from my life. I was deeply hurt. I couldn't believe that he would abandon me so swiftly once I became sick, after all the ways I'd demonstrated my love and loyalty to him. What kind of stupid pills did I take? More lies to myself because I liked him and was seeking a man in my life. Later, I cringed at the painful memories whenever anyone mentioned his name. I never wanted to see him again.

I felt he owed me. But I was wrong, despite his poor behavior. You see, since then, I've learned that no one owes me anything. And every individual is working his or her own spiritual path at the level he or she can. It's up to me to recognize individuals who treat me the way I deserve to be treated, and to let the others go. Only God can give me the kind of unconditional love I was looking for with Sam. Most importantly, I learned that the love I was seeking was inside of me all the time.

In the following months, I began to finally learn the art of loving myself. I also learned to eliminate from my life people who were toxic to me. These were just two of the many lessons I learned on my journey into healing.

Chapter Fifteen
Money Matters

"Most of the important things in the world have been accomplished by people who have kept trying when there seemed to be no hope at all."

~ Dale Carnegie

In 1985, I purchased a co-op apartment in southeast Washington, D.C. I was able to pay it off in just three years... leaving me free to spend my money on whatever I wanted. While I was always timely about paying my bills, I wasn't much of a saver.

One of the most interesting things about having a chronic illness is the fact that it touches every aspect of your life, including your financial resources. When you get ill, you need more money to live on. I didn't have it.

As a child, money was the source of much tension in my family. While my father gave lip service to "working hard and saving money," we didn't really learn about allowances, budgeting or saving. He made a good salary as a bricklayer, and talked a lot about money, but we never saw any... literally. He tucked it away, folded it up and hid it away from prying eyes. He would dangle the promise of money as a reward for running his bath water or untying his bootlaces and promise to pay us later. Our resentment grew when he gave money to our playmates for no apparent reason. My parents argued over money. My father hid it from my mother who was waiting to pay overdue bills. In effect, my early exposure to money was that it was the root of all evil.

We grew up thinking we were poor and felt that relatives looked down on us with sympathy. But looking back I realize we had enough. We didn't go hungry. We were clean and well dressed. We even had dance lessons! It wasn't that we didn't have enough money. It was that it was misplaced and mismanaged. As an adult, I became a prompt bill payer but poor saver who always wanted more when it came to money. I spent it as fast as I made it.

Before I got sick, I was enjoying my income and spending like there was no tomorrow. I remember a $1300 phone bill once that I easily paid because I had the funds available. Now it's scary to me that I had that much money to give away to the phone company. I could have used it towards a down payment for a home. I wasted so much that I wish I had now.

Part Two
Changes

"Do not go where the path may lead, go instead where there is no path and leave a trail."
~ Ralph Waldo Emerson

I have learned that my journey into healing from Scleroderma would require healing of my mind, body, and spirit. I view the physical dis-ease as a manifestation of the unhealthy attitudes I learned as a child and the ways I acted upon them throughout adulthood. I knew that I could not get well unless I dealt with the harsh reality that my healing was my responsibility. I could no longer look at the doctors and expect them to create a miracle cure.

Not feeling Good Enough all those years led me down a path of allowing people to take advantage of me, not letting go of bad habits and relationships, not accepting responsibility for what I wanted. Despite my love of God, I didn't trust that He would heal me. There were many, many components involved in the healing process and they centered around my mind, my body and my spirit. And so I embraced this holistic approach by determining to make healthy changes that would nourish all of me.

I had to let go of all the things in the past that had imprisoned me. I demanded my freedom from past fears, hurt, guilt, emotional traumas and mental anguish. I was reminded of God's love and commitment to me in a song by Richard Smallwood. "Stand still and look up, knowing that God is going to show up," he sang. "He is standing by." These words touched my spirit so deeply I played the song over and over while my tears flowed. "There is healing for your sorrow. Healing for your pain. Healing for your spirit. There's shelter from the rain. God is a healer. Earth has no sorrow that Heaven cannot heal. There is no situation that you are going through that God cannot fix."

They were comforting words. I thought about how my body and spirit had been broken, and the suffering I endured alone day and night, with no end in sight. So often I had prayed for death and was tempted many a night to commit suicide. But the healer had never left my side.

Chapter Sixteen

Social Security... Scare City

"In any moment of decision, the best thing you can do is the right thing, the next best thing is the wrong thing, and the worst thing you can do is nothing."

~ Theodore Roosevelt

In September 1996, I left my job at the hospital. My stress there was increasing daily. I had wanted to leave much earlier, but I let fear keep me shackled there. After seven months of listening to the urgency in my inner voice, I decided to feel the fear and do it anyway.

I was in denial of my illness. I wasn't thinking straight. I was exhausted from the stress and strain and thought I'd make ends meet somehow with my free-lance voice-over work. If I concentrated hard enough, I was sure I could make a living at the career I'd always planned.

So I simply resigned without any explanation. I didn't explore my right to my employee disability insurance. As a result, I lost monies that were owed to me. Of the $12,000 I had earned in the employee investment program, I recouped just $9,000 after early withdrawal penalties and taxes. I used it to live on, pay off credit cards and other balances due, as well as maintenance fees due to the co-op where I lived.

As my health deteriorated, I sought out assistance from the Supplementary Security Income (SSI) Washington, D.C. office a needs-based program for those who are not insured. I was having a particularly painful day when I went into the office for my eligibility interview. I coughed and gagged the entire time. While the interviewer was supportive and sympathetic, SSI turned me down anyway. They said I was not eligible because of my retirement pay-off from work, which I had long since exhausted paying overdue bills.

I also had no health insurance. My sister Kim kept urging me to apply for Social Security Disability (SSD) and so when I finally stumbled upon the excellent information from The Arthritis Foundation, I did apply. It took me a full week to complete the required forms and narratives... two full days to write and a week in bed to recover from the stress. Even though it took a terrible toll on my health, my preparation did pay off because I was approved on my first attempt, unlike the experience of so many others.

I learned from this experience to begin listening to my body. Even though I wanted desperately to operate at my normal level, I planned my days more carefully, incorporating fewer activities. I prepared for potentially stressful days with extra rest beforehand or afterwards. I stopped working as an extra on movie sets due to the long hours they required. I finally learned that the money wasn't worth the down time that would follow these activities.

My poor saving habits seemed magnified now. I thought back to all the money I'd spent shopping for clothes to feel good about how I looked. The money I spent every two weeks to maintain the short and sassy hair cut and perm I loved. What did it all matter if I couldn't afford to feed myself? Or pay my co-op maintenance fee?

Fortunately, my car disability insurance allowed me to suspend car payments. When we're healthy, it's hard to imagine a time when we might need the disability insurance on our credit cards or car. But I highly recommend that individuals carry this insurance. The pennies it costs to buy are nothing compared to the potential benefit in case of crisis.

While I was receiving state Medicaid assistance that included coverage for doctor, dental, hospital, and pharmacy, my many medications were expensive and unaffordable on my $852 in SSD benefits. My financial challenges made me increasingly frustrated and angry.

It was a devastating emotional roller coaster. Just when I most needed to marshall all my energy for healing, I felt called upon to complete a marathon of questionable nature. It became clear that only those with the most stamina and persistence would win social security benefits. It requires stamina for waiting and filling out forms for government benefits. Persistence to keep on keeping on, despite poor treatment by government representatives for social services and the belief that the aid will come in time to meet your financial obligations.

HOW TO APPLY FOR DISABILITY

According to Jill Jordan Sieder in her article "The Disability Dance," published in Arthritis Today magazine, 65% of people who apply for Social Security disability (SSD) are initially denied! Of those who persevere through the appeals process, more than half eventually win an award.

While it can also be an emotionally draining process, this financial aid can be critical if you have a chronic illness and really can't work. Prepare well ahead of time by contacting the Arthritis Foundation (www.arthritis.org) to request their handbook on how to apply for social security disability. You can also read Jill Jordan Sieders' article series by logging on to their website and searching on "disability insurance."

Contact the Social Security Administration to learn how much money you have paid into social security so you know what you can claim for disability. It's also important to know that you can schedule a telephone interview instead of an office interview if you prefer.

Ask someone to assist you in completing the application and proofread it for you before you send it to the Social Security Administration. Send it in promptly but expect to wait three to four months for an initial response to your request.

I'd feel relieved to receive the small annual increases in benefits so I could pay my rent and utilities. But each time I diligently reported to the Department of Health and Human Services (DHS) any small amount of financial assistance I received from my Money Angels, the state would reduce the amount of my food stamps by the amount I reported. Then they would raise it again later, but lower it because they counted my unsold co-op apartment in Washington, D.C as income although I couldn't rent it under the terms of the co-op agreement, nor could I afford the maintenance fees I owed.

This saga brought me much shame and embarrassment. In fact, I had a physical setback in my healing after each interaction with a government agency representative. I lived in fear that my services would be cut off at the whim of an insensitive social services or SSD representative. The system felt abusive. It encourages people to withhold financial information as they struggle to survive and punishes those who are truthful. I felt I was often at the mercy of government workers who are quick to state rules and regulations and slower to show compassion and caring. Today I can recognize their actions as fear-based, as if they know they are just one paycheck away from standing in the shoes of people like me. Perhaps it's a kind of shield or armor against anxiety to act as if you are insensitive to the plight of a fellow human being. Doctors… government workers… even some friends. They don't want to catch what you've got!

And so it went. Exhilaration at receiving a notification that my SSD would be increased for 2001. Deep despair shortly thereafter upon receiving a letter stating that my disability payments would be cancelled immediately, since the government deemed I'd been gainfully employed in 1997. Two years earlier, I had already cleared up confusion with the Social Security Administration about how I had accurately reported this residual income that I'd earned from acting. But no one would listen. They cut off my benefits and I was forced to start back at the beginning and reapply. I was near death at the time and submitted my claim feeling that they hoped for my death so they wouldn't have to pay me back the tax dollars I'd paid into Social Security during my working days.

I lost my Medicare (federal health insurance) too. So a surgery that they told me was approved, was denied after I had it in January 2001. There were many instances where I was given false information. I had to make appeals to reinstate my benefits. I grew so tired of fighting for what was rightfully mine.

After six months of appeals and letters to my congressional representatives and Social Security administrators, my benefits were finally reinstated. If it hadn't been for my friend Sheyla, who took over all my bills at that time, I'm not sure what would have become of me. I thank God He placed her in the right place at the right time.

Just as I was celebrating my hard-won victory of having my benefits reinstated, a large brown envelope from SSA showed up informing me that I now owed them $22,000 for overpayments they'd made because of the 1997 residual income issue I'd just resolved! They planned to subtract $300 in benefits monthly from August 2001 until the year 2009! Oh... and they stopped Medicare coverage once again.

I was incredulous. I knew it was futile to try again. And although I did, they ignored my explanations. How long was I doomed to ride this scary roller coaster?

This system does not work to help those who desperately need it. I know a man in Washington, D.C. who is feigning an illness that nets him approximately $3000 per month in Social Security benefits. I hear he enjoys a good life now. I doubt he will be approached about overpayments, since SSD seems to be fairly busy harassing people like me who really need the assistance. I wish that my story was unusual... but it's not. When will our government turn their attention to this broken system?

Still, learning to advocate for my rights was another important beginning for me in learning that I was Good Enough.

Chapter Seventeen
The Pacific Northwest: A Breath of Fresh Air

"What do I have to lose?"

~ E. McDonald James, my diamond

When I decided I needed more breathing room and clean air. As my lungs hardened with Scleroderma, the smog of the urban city suffocated me. Intuitively I felt it was important to move to a more pristine, healing environment and I was drawn to the Pacific Northwest. I relocated to Seattle, near my sister Kim. At the Puget Sound, I was able to welcome complete healing into my mind, body, and soul.

I had no funds to do this, but I knew deep inside of my heart that I needed to get there. I felt that God would help me if I could find a way. And He did. It turned out that Social Security Disability (SSD) owed me retroactive funds, which was almost exactly what I needed to buy a plane ticket and ship my car and personal belongings.

I believe this was not only a blessing, but also God's signal that I was doing His will. But I still wondered how I'd manage the huge cost of living increase on my small monthly budget from disability. My rent was six times higher in Seattle than my D.C. co-op fee had been, eating up most of my monthly check, not including utilities, food, costly medication, and any other expenses.

But I was increasingly trusting God so I took a leap of faith and prayed for a miracle. I also took responsibility for helping myself by applying for Medicaid. I completed all the forms as honestly as I could. But once I reported that I owned a co-op apartment in Washington, D.C. that was currently for sale, my application was denied as this was considered "income." To make matters worse, until it sold, I was responsible for paying a monthly maintenance fee on the apartment that I couldn't afford.

My co-op neighbor and long-time friend Pam W. was the first of what I later came to call my "money angels." After seven years of living on the same floor as polite acquaintances in Washington, D.C., Pam W. and her daughter reached out to me and made me a part of their daily lives when they learned what I was going through. Pam W. was calm and wise. There were so many times when she sat with me in my pain while whispering those soothing words, "It's okay."

So I wasn't surprised ~ but blessed ~ when Pam W. granted me an extended loan and paid the maintenance fees on my apartment. After years of being the one who was always there for others and feeling so alone, things shifted. I noticed that I increasingly trusted God, did what I could to help myself, and accepted the rest. Support from so many friends and strangers suddenly came my way. In fact more than 40 "money angels" sent money to me just to help.

I continued to fight for food stamps. A state social services caseworker reviewed, granted, rescinded, and reinstated food stamp benefits so many times I was almost afraid to open my mailbox... all because of my apartment that wouldn't sell across the country.

Each month, I didn't know if I would have benefits or not. As I rode this emotional seesaw, I worried about my lack of health insurance. I knew my health was worsening and I needed to be hospitalized. Even though I knew I had a right to be treated even if I didn't have health insurance, I felt ashamed. I was fearful of being treated like so many of the ER patients I remembered who were taking advantage of the system, so I didn't seek out care. And what if a doctor recommended a scary procedure for some new life threatening medical condition? I was physically and emotionally spent. My mind was clouded by the pain and medication side effects so I wasn't making good decisions.

Now I know that it's important to feel the fear and shame and do it anyway. The law says you have a right to seek care and are also eligible for Medicaid when you need it. As for fears about what a doctor "might say," more information is usually better than less. Sometimes no treatment options sound like good ones, but nonetheless, we must choose a course of action consciously.

My illness progressed. Eventually it hurt to smile and eat. Sometimes my mouth would stick together due to the lack of saliva due to Sjorgrens Syndrome, a disorder that can create dryness of the mouth and a myriad of other symptoms. One of the hardest things about my declining health had been losing the gift of my singing voice. I wasn't sure what happened, but it happened suddenly.

It was January 1997, after I'd just completed background vocals on a video/CD project for the gospel quartet The Canton Spirituals. It was the coldest day of the decade just 14 degrees and we had performed in a packed church with the outside door slightly ajar to allow the cables for the recording to extend to the truck outside.

Our holding area had no heat and the concert producers hadn't anted up any hot coffee or tea to keep us warm as we waited to perform. But that's gospel music for you... always on a tight budget.

I was miserably cold, but my passion for the art of music kept my feet glued to the ground. The moment the concert ended, I opened my mouth to answer someone and nothing came out. I could not talk. I had lost my voice. For three weeks I was in bed and could only whisper. That was the last time I was able to sing. I'm grateful it was recorded. In fact, the album and associated video went on to top the gospel quartet charts in 1998... for this I earned $50, a free meal, and the death of my beautiful mezzo-soprano voice.

I learned that we should always use the talents God grants us for we don't know when we might lose them. It is so painful to know that I once performed with the best in the business... background vocals for Michael Jackson... trading lines with Kathleen Turner and Suzanne Sommers in their movie Serial Mom... doubling for actress, Sandra Coleman, in Meteor Man, starring Robert

Towson, Eddie Griffin, Marla Gibbs, James Earle Jones, Don Cheadle and many others.

I wish I had cherished my health and nurtured my talents more when I had the opportunity and hadn't let my worries about being Not Good Enough stand in the way. But perhaps there will still be a second chance... as my energy and vitality continue to rise.

I was so desperate to find answers for my deteriorating health that I enrolled in a Johns Hopkins research study in October 1997. I felt so sick that I was in no mood to be a guinea pig for research, but my empty wallet was a powerful motivator. Participating in the study paid $250!

The study would examine samples of the T-cells in my lungs and cultivate them so researchers could better understand their role in the hardening of the lungs in Scleroderma patients. By then, I had developed a host of new symptoms and arrived sporting a terrible cough, shortness of breath, mouth sores, itchy, dry skin; and a complete loss of my singing voice. I had esophageal stricture, which made it difficult for anything to go down my throat.

Since the procedure involved sedation, I was downright scared of choking on my own saliva or having my lungs collapse while the doctors poked around taking samples and running tests. Because Scleroderma patients are already in so much pain, all tests and procedures are particularly painful and difficult.

I was a frightened patient. During the procedure, I had a major coughing spell and asked a nurse to help me clear my lung passages with a sharp rap on my back. She refused and I got angry. I was anesthetized at the time, but I was in a mean frame of mind and threatened her. I apologized afterwards.

I wish that more caregivers in health care could find the compassion for patients that they would no doubt offer their own loved ones. In similar circumstances, nurses, like doctors, so often shield themselves from these feelings in their rush to move through procedures... forgetting that each patient is a vulnerable, frightened human being. Increasingly, hospitals ~ anxious to attract more patients to their facility ~ are sending surveys to past inpatients to benchmark patient satisfaction. They seem so surprised that their patient satisfaction scores soar when they use the little kindnesses humans share with each other. A gentle smile and touch on the hand is sometimes a far move effective way to quell a patient's anxiety than anti-anxiety medication. Why are they so reluctant to offer it?

The results of the research study indicated that my lungs had fibrosis; they were hardening and not functioning as they should. They also found a few polyps on my vocal cords, which explained why I was not able to sing. (Ah, the amazement of modern technology!) Again the doctor recommended steroidal medication immediately to slow down the progression of the fibrosis. Again, I refused the treatment plan, but I got paid!

Chapter Eighteen
Tears, Fears, and Phobias

"You must do the things
you think you cannot do."

~ Eleanor Roosevelt

My emotions ran high as I weighed the risks and benefits of a lung transplant procedure that was eventually recommended. This is also when my phobia of bathrooms really peaked. My own bathroom was frightening enough, but I'd do almost anything to avoid a public bathroom.

So it was with terrible chagrin that I dashed in and out of the public restroom at the University of Washington Medical Center, trying hard to shield my eyes from the sight of my own waste. I was there to meet with a lung transplant specialist to determine if I was a good candidate for the transplant procedure. While I was initially in favor of the procedure, I eventually declined after examining all the "ifs" involved. "If" my body would accept or reject it. "If " I could somehow afford it financially. "If" the Scleroderma would eventually attack the new lungs. "If " I was mentally prepared for all the "ifs." After careful consideration, I declined and decided I wanted to live out whatever days were left with as much unnecessary suffering as possible.

But the visit to the public restroom at the medical center seemed to jumpstart my bathroom phobia. It had first germinated during my days working in hospital emergency rooms, but seemed to be gaining ground until I had to steel myself just to walk into a bathroom.

While I'd been preoccupied with the filth I saw in hospitals, my distaste for bathrooms didn't become a phobia until my Scleroderma diagnosis. After I became ill, the combination of my dis-ease and medications found me frequently vomiting in the bathroom or rushing for the toilet when at times I lost control of my bowels. I became afraid to look at myself and my waste. It seemed an ugly manifestation of how the dis-ease had ravaged my body inside and out.

I began compulsively closing the toilet seat lid and telling myself I was just following the principles of Feng Shui, which said toilet lids should be closed to protect one's fortune from "going down the drain." (What fortune?) But then I had to concede something more was going on as I started closing the door to the bathroom as well and complaining about going in there to my sister and friends. I kept imagining an awful stench that was not there. I wanted to clean it but could not and asked my sister to take over this task for me.

But I told myself I was on a journey into healing and self-reflection and these behaviors were not normal. So on a day when I felt particularly energetic, I decided to clean both bathrooms. I donned a facemask and gloves, and grabbed the cleanser and prepared myself to do battle, when my toothbrush slipped to the floor. I was overwhelmed by the thought of my precious toothbrush on that filthy floor. So I threw it away and continued my crusade.

After the mirrors, I attacked the biggie: the toilet. But when I saw some pale brown spots on the back of the seat, I scrubbed frantically. Before I knew it, I was in the midst of a full-fledged anxiety attack. My heart pounded and tears fell from my eyes. But I was determined to remove the stains. My face flushed as I cried uncontrollably.

I gave up, wailing as if I was in great pain, with an overwhelming need to be away from the bathroom. I sat on the bed watching myself in the mirror as my flushed face continued to cry. I fled the bathroom and bawled at my desk in the living room.

I felt like a frightened, confused child with nowhere to turn. Finally, I called my old friend Pam W. who had always been so adept at calming me. But even she couldn't help. I decided I needed to go through the experience and see it through to the end wherever it took me. I curled into a fetal position begging God for answers as I cried and talked to my Aunt Jo on the phone. But this time I didn't let myself be drawn into the emotion I was expressing. I watched it as an impartial observer and coached myself through it. I listened to my inner self in silence.

Now I know this is a phobia I developed. While some people fear spiders or snakes and can choose to avoid them, I know that I will have to fully accept toilets in my life!

Chapter Nineteen
My Angels

"Thank you for your love
and concern."

~ "Miss Daisy Doodle"
Virginia Yarborough, my mother

Since my move to Washington, I have cultivated so many wonderful new friendships and been blessed by so many angels near and far away. A gift that God gave me on my healing journey.

I began to feel God's presence more vividly because of Scleroderma. He led me to people who helped rescue me from myself. Support from my sister, Kim, and her husband, John, who facilitated their friend, Pam Barnes, becoming my caretaker through the state. My Seattle neighbors, Kay and Stan, who would call or knock when they didn't see me for a few days. It was such a blessing to experience this kind of love.

I feel that God was leading me through a dis-ease to test me. If I opened myself and followed the messages Spirit sent me through people, music, and dreams, the pain would wash away and I might gain a second chance at life.

It was while I was weighing the decision of my lung transplant that Sharon, a mere acquaintance at the time, felt divinely inspired to write the poem "Angel with a Broken Wing," reprinted at the beginning of this book.

When I asked her what compelled her to write such beautiful verse for someone she hardly knew, Sharon told me she felt divinely inspired to offer words that would reunite my body and spirit. She believed I was one of God's angels placed here on earth to serve a purpose, but that it was not my time to depart and I needed encouragement.

One of the early ways I reached for support was by learning how to use a computer and share the ups and downs of Scleroderma with other individuals and Scleroderma victims via the Internet. Before my diagnosis, I was only at home to shower and sleep. Afterwards, it was difficult to be homebound. A little voice inside told me to buy a fax machine and computer. So I did, even though I wasn't gainfully employed then. Over time, I learned to listen closely to this little voice. It was Spirit, deep inside me, and I could count on it to guide me.

Many old friends helped me on journey towards computer and Internet literacy as I struggled to reach out to the world. In fact, I named my first computer GwenDolyn, after my oldest sister who is a computer educator. Later, when I relocated to Seattle, I named my new computer Cup-O-Coffee, after my other sister Nancy who loves coffee.

After my move, it was a blessing to stay connected to friends and family back home via e-mail when I felt lonely. Soon I branched out and made Scleroderma cyber friends that lived worldwide. The Internet was truly a lifeline to others who rode the same physical and emotional roller coaster that I did. They really understood what I was going through. These Internet angels were very loving and supportive.

I often sent out progress reports about my condition to all my Internet Angels—my family, Cuzin Connections (cousins), The Puppies (my nieces and nephews), my Prayer Warriors (via the Internet worldwide), and Borders Buddies (friends from Borders Bookstore), SD connections (Scleroderma patients) ~ and was overjoyed at all the responses I received. When I had a medical decision to make, I would consult with all these angels. They always came through with good advice, prayers, information, and encouragement.

However, in the summer of 2000, the Scleroderma had spread to my brain. I had contracted CNS vasculitis (the blood vessels to my brain were constricted) and the pain attacked me with a vengeance. I was disoriented, dizzy, confused and in constant, severe pain. When I finally went to the emergency room, doctors told me they suspected a cranial bleed, but the MRI showed nothing. I walked around in this fog of constant pain for a month on high doses of pain medication.

ON INTERNET SUPPORT GROUPS

Connecting with other individuals who share a similar diagnosis via the Internet can be tremendously empowering, informative, and life sustaining. Chances are, no matter what illness you struggle with, there is a community on the Internet of people just like you.

When you register for a list serve, you can receive individual e-mails or a "digest" of daily posts from other subscribers while still maintaining as much privacy as you want to. (See Yahoogroups.com to find or start a list) Typically, e-mail addresses are not revealed. Some subscribers prefer to simply read others' posts but not post themselves.

You will no doubt meet individuals with much wisdom and experience to share and may later help mentor others with a new diagnosis. Remember though to be cautious about taking medical advice from list subscribers, just as you would from friends in your own life. Everyone's experience is unique!

I began to prepare for my death. I gave away possessions. I told people goodbye and that I loved them. I asked a social worker to make arrangements for hospice care. While Dr. Hillson had respected my decision not to take steroidal medication earlier in my illness, now she recommended that I reconsider my decision because I risked a stroke. I could accept that I was dying, but I couldn't bear the pain, so after five years of resisting the Prednisone, I elected to take it, along with Cytoxin, to control the inflammation of the blood vessels in my brain.

During these dark days in August 2000, another angel walked into my life. In fact, she saved my life. My friend Sheyla, who I'd first met at a seminar in Silver Spring, MD in 1990, showed up on my doorstep and made my house a home. She'd been living with a friend in Maryland, but came to me with what she described as a desperate inner knowing of my impending demise. She was sent by God to help me mend my broken wing. For two years, Sheyla brought life and companionship to my home in Washington State when I most needed it and I am so grateful. She was also my money angel, taking over all the bills when I was financially destitute while fighting with the Social Security Administration over monies due me. She left her family, siblings, and children to save my life. A gifted visionary, she is a blessing to all who meet her.

I think perhaps all the angels in my life have been sent by my grandfather to watch over me… that perhaps he's returning the favor. You see, when I was a young girl, Kim and I used to spend summers riding all over God's creation with my maternal grandfather, an accomplished Baptist minister in North Carolina, as he drove to and from the five churches he pastored. Since we'd all have to wake early and return late, we'd often be bored and exhausted.

Sometimes my grandfather liked to catnap at the steering wheel. Kim and I were petrified he might cause a terrible accident and we'd all go to heaven before our time. But it seemed that God had control of the car and kept us safe. I prayed that one day God would allow me to drive for my grandfather so he could relax and really sleep.

My prayer was answered, but not in the way I expected. Be careful what you pray for because prayers may be answered in ways you never dreamed! When I finally got my driver's license at sixteen, my grandfather had fallen ill to cancer. It was difficult seeing him suffer with no way to ease his pain. But there was one thing that I could do for him. I could drive. Although I never got the chance to drive him around, I was there to drive at the most important time… before he left this earth. By driving my mother and grandmother back and forth to see their beloved in the hospital thirty miles away, it was my honor and pleasure to bridge the gap between distance and death.

So my childhood prayer was answered. I was his driving angel. And I believe that when I became sick, he sent much more than a driving angel. He asked God to send an army of all kinds of angels to me.

I believe in "karma," the spiritual law of cause and effect. Others may say, "What goes around comes around." Whatever you choose to call it, this spiritual law is an exacting one, so it is important to pay attention to what you send out into the universe. Your actions, deeds, and words will come back to you in the same way you offered them to the world. This is another of the many lessons I learned on my journey into healing. I'm honored to share it with you as you create healing in your own life.

In my life, I learned that angels are everywhere. When my sister Nancy needed financial assistance for a plane ticket to come visit, she posted her need to see me to friends and family on the Internet and was overwhelmed with their responses. She received over $500 of love offerings to speed her to Seattle to help me during a difficult time. Angels surround us, but sometimes we must ask for their help.

While there was a time when I briefly followed the teachings of a religion that discouraged prayers without permission, now I welcome prayers from wherever they come. I believe they are a powerful force and that prayer speeds my healing. In fact, my name has been added to church prayer lists all over the country. I felt the power of these prayers.

I also joined the Evergreen Chapter Support Group of the National Scleroderma Foundation for local support. At my first meeting, I was impressed by the cohesiveness of the group and their enthusiasm for helping each other. They helped me to recognize the deep depression I was in at the time and to seek out a therapist and anti-depressants which both helped tremendously. It wasn't long before members of the group learned about my broadcasting experience and appointed me to the board of directors to help increase awareness about Scleroderma.

Chapter Twenty
Facing the Demons Inside

"If you are on the road to nowhere,
find another road."

~ Ashanti proverb

When my sister-in law's sister, Meta, died of AIDS, it made me consider the suicide demons that I'd been entertaining myself after fighting depression and suicidal tendencies for months. I felt these were not my true feelings, and worked to fight them away. I sat down and wrote this poem...

NAMELESS

Demons, why do you bother me?
I want to live. Can't you see?
There is a plan for my life that is divine.
Leave me be. I'll be just fine.

My life is worth more than what you seek.
My soul you want , that card I peeped.
You want me to fail. You want me to fall.
The power of God I constantly call.

I admit your offer sounds tempting,
I am in so much awful pain.
But I must fight your power again and again.
Demons seeking to devour and destroy,

Playing with me like I was a Christmas toy.
In and out, out and in.
When did this dangerous game begin?
What's more is when and how will it ever end?

My soul seeks solace comfort and rest.
To wait on God feels to be what's best.
When it is my time, for home I'll head.
Won't need your help, just love instead.

Demons, leave me alone. Go back to your home.
And wait for a soul that wants to be less than whole.

After writing the poem, I began to talk about my feelings more with people who loved me. And the more I talked and shared with others, the weaker the urge to end my life became. Suppressing my feelings the way I always had as a child would drive my distorted thinking and deepen my pain. I felt my healing power more when I talked it out.

I had been spending lots of time at the Borders book store in Federal Way, Washington so it seemed natural to enter my poem in their poetry contest. When I won first prize on June 12, 2002, I was thrilled to know my poem had touched someone so deeply! A few weeks later, I was coordinating an "Afternoon of Creative Awareness" for National Scleroderma Awareness Month. I shared my poem and music on that special afternoon. I felt giddy from all the attention I received during my presentation, which many described as "powerful, "and after struggling so long with feeling unattractive, I felt truly radiant in my new dress!

Chapter Twenty One
Lifestyle Changes

"Your vision will become clear
only when you look into your heart.
Who looks outside, dreams. Who
looks inside, awakens."

~ Carl Jung

As my spirits lifted, I was inspired to make more lifestyle changes. It was not enough that I had changed my hairstyle, my phone number, my address, my list of friends and acquaintances, my daily routine, and my environmental surroundings. I had to change my eating habits.

I decided to give my poor body every nutritional advantage to jumpstart healing so I also added vitamin supplements to my daily routine. On the advice of my acupuncturist, I stopped eating dairy products, as well as fast and fried foods. This was a tall order for me, but the abundance of healthy food choices in Washington State made it easier. The Seattle area grocers catered to more holistic lifestyle choices. I began to eat more soy, tofu, fruits, and vegetables.

There was also a great deal of inner work that I needed to do. The real me needed to take a long look in that mirror again to see who she was and who she was about to become as a result of Scleroderma. I began to spend time with myself mindfully through daily meditation and ate my meals in silence with full awareness to keep myself more centered and balanced. I learned how to become an objective observer who monitored my actions and reactions to people and events. I paid attention to what I was feeling and why.

One of the things that helped me in my quest for self-knowledge was daily journaling. By making a regular practice of writing down my thoughts and feelings, I began to finish thoughts so they were no longer circling around in my head ceaselessly. Upon reviewing my writings over time, I noticed subtle progress in physical changes and in my psyche.

I also began eliminating any stressors from my life and started to notice how many little things contributed to my mood. My appetite for self-knowledge grew greater and fueled my desire for healing. I read more on alternative lifestyles, self-healing, and spirituality.

Scleroderma changed the shape of my eyes both physically and spiritually. It changed my outlook on life. I could now see people and situations in a different light and I realized what was important. I had wasted so much time trying to live for others. I saw how much of my life was a show, an act, a lie. I realized how much I had lied to myself as well as others.

Chapter Twenty Two
Letting Go and Moving On

"The best way to predict your future is to create it."

~ Unknown

One of the things I came to face was that I had never moved through my grief for my lost love for Kenney. I hadn't trusted in the power of love and so lost his.

So after months and years of denial about the importance of this relationship, I called him when I was sleepless in the early morning to tell him that I had never stopped loving him. This was an important step in my spiritual healing because I called to share my own truth with no expectation about his response. And when I did this, I felt a heavy burden lifted from my shoulders. It was a humbling experience and I didn't prolong the call. He told me that true love never dies before we ended our conversation.

I thought back to all the years he'd pursued our true love and I had been blind to his importance in my life. Even after we broke up, he was the first person I thought of to share a hurt with, a special event, an important happening in my life. Ironically, after the call, I made a trip to the bathroom and released old waste there too.

I've since noticed that whenever I confronted a truth in my life, this type of physical release would accompany it. Then a symptom of my disease would fade away. I believe my experience speaks to the important link between the physiological and emotional components in healing.

As a Kwanza gift in December 1999, I asked my family to apologize to him for the way they had treated him... and this too was healing for Kenney, my family, and me. They made amends for the part they played in our lost love. Most importantly, my mother understood the significance of my request and went far beyond a simple apology. She invited Kenney over to speak with him in person. When she called him on New Year's Day, he came over the same day. It was such a healing gesture. God is so good.

I even reconciled with Sam eventually. Remember Sam, for whom I held such bitter feelings? He called out of the blue when I was visiting my family one Spring. While my initial reaction was to suppress my anger, I gave him my e-mail address as he requested and allowed myself to let go of the past, and be open to forgiveness.

I never expected to hear from him again, so I was surprised when he sent me a letter of apology. I had never thought he could be capable of acknowledging wrongdoings, much less apologize for them. But he did, and it made all the difference, healing a deep wound that had festered in my heart for so many years.

Sam kept in touch regularly. He was now a single father who regaled me with stories and photos of his beautiful five-year old daughter. I kept waiting for signs of his old behaviors but he proved to be sincere in his friendship.

In fact, when he learned I was coming home to Washington, DC to be with my family during my father's fatal illness, he offered me keys to his co-op apartment to use as a getaway for rest and relaxation. I took him up on his offer and really enjoyed my home away from home, away from home. He left kind notes for me and money for food. It was wonderful to experience his generosity, and my ability to accept a new dynamic in our relationship.

He was so different these days... sensitive, caring, kind, and compassionate. During my three-month stay in DC, he made me feel like someone really cared about me for a change. He treated me like a friend, and kept in constant contact. I was not sure if it was that he felt that he owed me for saving his life, or that it was genuine love. Had he changed? Or had this always been his persona? Maybe when I met him in the early '90's, he was going through a healing of his own dis-ease. Whatever happened to him, it was all good.

Chapter Twenty Three
On Healing vs. a Cure

"As a man thinketh, so is he."

~ Unknown

I believe that we create our world with our words and thoughts. Do you know that 85% of dis-ease is mental, while the other 15% is the physical manifestation of what is in our heads?

Watch your thoughts and the patterns that you create. If you think sick, you will be sick. If you think poor, you will be poor. If you think ugly, or fat or undeserving; you will have that in your life. I learned this the hard way and had to reprogram myself to think differently and become a different person. It takes time and effort, but if you really want healing, it is worth the effort.

Positive affirmations can be quite empowering as you say them out loud to yourself. Your mind, spirit, and body will believe what you tell it. Imagine yourself well, happy, healthy, worthy and blessed. And hold on to those positive thoughts. Try these:

I am worthy.
I am loving and accept myself completely as I am.
I am a peaceful, loving and forgiving human being.
I accept all my feelings and love myself as I am.
I use all my experiences to learn and grow.

Talk to your body and tell it what you want or don't want. Since your body replaces all cells within a year, why not ask your cells to replace the old ones with vibrant, healthy cells?

Surround yourself with positive people that make you feel supported. Choose doctors that are sensitive to your special needs and emotions. Find a qualified therapist to help you deal with emotional issues and creating meaningful change in your life.

It's important to understand there is a difference between being healed and being cured. In Christiane Northrup's book, Women's Bodies, Women's Wisdom, she explains that:

"Healing is a natural process and is within the power of everyone. Curing, which is what doctors are called upon to do, usually consists of an external treatment; medication or surgery is used to mask or eliminate symptoms. This external treatment does not necessarily address the factors that contributed to the symptoms in the first place. Healing goes deeper than curing and must always come from within: It addresses the imbalance that underlies the symptoms. Healing brings together the often hidden aspects of a person's life as they relate to their illness. Healing is different from curing, though curing and the restoration of the physical function may accompany healing. One can be healed completely and go on to die of her illness."

Northrup continues: "This concept is often missing from treatises on holistic medicine. Healing and death are not mutually exclusive: We need to accept death as a natural part of a process that is much bigger and more mysterious than we realize. Pat Reiss, who works with many of our patients' dreams and body symptoms says, "The bigger meaning of healing is a 'whole-ing,' a filling out of missing pieces in a person's life. Sometimes this may even mean facing death in a more fully realized way. Certainly it is an opportunity to come more deeply and fully into life."

Said another way, Reiki practitioners like to stress that healing is not just the removal of symptoms. Healing is a full and complete resolution of the causes of the dis-ease. Healing is returning to a state of alignment with your Higher Self or true way of being."[7]

---

[7] "Using Reiki for Healing" by David Herron, http://reiki.7gen.com/doreiki.htm.

I began participating in "The Psychic Showcase," a twice weekly meeting of spiritual individuals interested in sharing their intuitive arts. I also began therapeutic counseling to better understand my emotional life. I learned that my gifts of the Spirit were real and not to fear them, but to use them as tools to help heal myself and the world.

HOW TO FIND THE RIGHT MENTAL HEALTH PRACTITIONER

Just as when you are choosing doctors, you must be an informed consumer when selecting a therapist. Here's how to find one who's right for you:

- Define what you are seeking from a therapist. Do you need grief counseling? Someone experienced in trauma? An expert on the emotional issues that come with chronic pain?

- Check the credentials of the therapist you choose and ask about their specializations. Psychologists hold doctorate degrees and so have the most education. Many, however, rely heavily on standardized paper and pencil testing for diagnosis and treatment, which can seem impersonal. Others, however, have long since dropped this practice in favor of more personal and flexible approaches. Marriage and family therapists (MFTs) are relationship experts and can be useful in addressing ways that your illness disrupts relationships with a spouse, your children, and your family. Licensed social workers (LSWs) may or may not have ANY counseling experience depending on the focus of their study... so ask.

- After you've identified a few candidates, ask each to set up a fifteen minute phone interview with you so you can learn more about their expertise and how they might help you. Your goal is to determine if this person seems like a good match, someone you feel you can open up with. Don't be shy about asking for a referral to another therapist they may know with more expertise in the areas where you need help. Be considerate of their time by keeping the call short since a good therapist won't bill you for this.

- At the initial session, explain your challenges as you understand them. Ask them about their potential treatment approach. Do they do cognitive behavioral therapy? Insight-based therapy? Do their opinions about when and how to use medication match your own? Every therapist brings unique experience and expertise. Asking questions will help you determine the best match for you.

Chapter Twenty Four
Integrating Allopathic Care and Natural Medicine

"Take the first step in faith.
You don't have to see the whole
staircase. Just take the first step."

~ Dr. Martin Luther King, Jr.

After experimenting with many pharmaceutical and alternative health care modalities, I found a way to integrate both. I used medical technology to observe changes in my body chemistry and natural medicine to make me feel better.

Even though I was seeing some of the best specialists in the country, each visit revealed distressing realities confirmed by data and tests. The medications they prescribed often eased the symptoms. And, while I needed to know the truth about how and where the dis-ease was ravaging my body, I was also buoyed by the messages of hope and healing I came to expect from Augusto Romano, my acupuncturist, at Kent Community Health Center.[8] He offered a welcome perspective on how to help my body heal that inspired me. His words were, "First we pray. Second we pray. Third we pray."

At one point, Dr. Jan Hillson, my rheumatologist, confirmed along with other specialists that my lungs had been attacked by Scleroderma resulting in substantial scarring and fibrosis on both lungs. They warned it would worsen and urged me to take Cytoxin (an immunosuppressant frequently used to treat cancer patients) to stop the spread of the fibrosis, although there were no guarantees about its efficacy or how my body would respond to potential side effects.

---

[8] In acupuncture, practitioners insert special needles into specific points or "meridians" of the body to stimulate the body's natural energy.

I felt more comfortable with acupuncture, chiropractic, and Reiki and so stubbornly refused the medication.[9] Later however, I did decide to take Cytoxin and Prednisone while I continued natural therapies. The natural therapies helped but so did the drugs. I believed that the combination of all that I did unlocked the healing within me. I looked forward to being alive and well for the new millennium. And my wish was granted. I was blessed to see a new century with a new lease on life.

[9] Reiki is an ancient, non-invasive healing technique that works to restore and balance the life force and in its simplest form, involved the practitioner placing his/her hands on the recipient with the intent of bringing healing.

Chapter Twenty Five
PathFindHer

"There's no such thing in anyone's life as an unimportant day."

~ Alexander Woollcott

In February 2000, I met an extraordinary woman, who'd I later come to call PathFindHer, because of her gift in helping others find their way in life. I met Kathie first at a meeting of the Psychic Showcase and again the next day when we serendipitously met in a group carpooling to a local TV show, "Northwest Afternoon," which featured a guest appearance of Dr. Phil.

Typically, I didn't like to commit to events before I knew how my health would be, but intuitively I felt this was important. Kathie approached me as I walked towards the car and told me she remembered me from the other night and felt a connection... that we would do something important together to make a difference.

By now I welcomed messages from Spirit and was receptive to her words. Sheyla had once approached me similarly and our first encounter had led to a lifelong friendship.

As Kathie and I talked on the way to the television station, I learned that she had her own gifts and talents and also suffered from an autoimmune disease. She considers herself a visionary artist and is well versed in the healing and spiritual arts. I was awed by her vast knowledge of culture, rituals and the unseen world of Spirit. She shared so much so freely that afternoon.

Our friendship blossomed over the coming months. I had long since learned to pay attention to signs and symbols so when she announced one day that Scleroderma would leave my body soon, I grew excited with anticipation.

She felt strongly that together we were destined to make important contributions to the world.

Spirit confirmed her statement shortly afterwards. During the intermission at a jazz concert we attended at Borders bookstore, I picked up a book about the meaning of names. When I looked up my name, I read: "This is a woman with a brave heart and a noble spirit. Her name gives her these qualities plus a sincere interest in other people's welfare. It is common to find Valerie involved in charitable or humanitarian causes. Her pet projects may involve medical or sociological research and she will be interested in finding cures for the ills that beset the world."[10]

Scleroderma is certainly one of the ills of the world. The moment took my breath away. Since then, I have not only published this book, but founded the Scleroderma Wings of Angels Foundation, which provides services and aid to individuals with Scleroderma so they can devote all of their energy to the important work of healing.

This also felt like another confirmation for me that my dis-ease would not last in my body much longer. I re-committed to my faith in God's will. I believe God wanted me to know that even though my history was full of Not Good Enough, those were my words... not His. God wanted me to be healthy, but also to value health and learn the lessons I would not heed. God wanted me to know my parents did the best they could in raising me and that they would never knowingly hurt me. God wanted me to know love in its purest form and so God sent me angels and genuine friendships. I have experienced limitless love.

God wanted me to learn how to live life fully and could only show me how by stopping me in my tracks as I raced through life making the same mistakes and disrespecting my mind, body, and spirit. God wanted me to share my pain with the world to let others know that impossible dreams can come true.

---

[10] The Hidden Truth Of Your Name: A Complete Guide To First Names And What They Say About The Real You" by The Nomenology Project.

Chapter Twenty Six
The Cure

"The manifestation of obedience is healing."

~ Jesse Duplantis, evangelist

Many messages from Spirit began to come to me. My friend Raymond told me my illness would inspire others and that God had a plan for my life. Other messages were revealed, but the main one was that I was getting the help I needed. All I had to do was ask. The bible states that,"You have not because you ask not." I asked Spirit for total healing.

One morning when I woke up, my body felt different... it seemed like a million pieces of glitter were lifting out of it. I felt something rise out of me and dissipate in the air. The feeling is hard to explain, but I felt something shift. I knew something was leaving my body that was important and it had a direct relation to healing.

Afterwards I felt lighter and I had more energy. When I took my sister to lunch the next day, she commented on how good I looked. "Almost normal," she said. It confirmed for me that the shift was real. Even a bank teller noted that I seemed to have more color in my face. I was elated because Spirit confirmed my healing twice that day.

With my medical history, I should now be crippled, in a wheel chair, and waiting to die. Instead, on September 5, 2001 my cure was validated medically. I was expecting the miracle, but was overcome when it actually occurred. On a routine medical visit to my rheumatologist Dr. Hillson, gave me the result of the blood test that confirmed that the incurable dis-ease that had ravaged my body for seven years was in fact gone!

While Dr. Hillson was also treating me for Sarcoidosis, the Scleroderma inexplicably went away.[11] My miracle came quietly. Dr. Hillson and I embraced each other with emotion when she confirmed there were no traces of Scleroderma present in my body. This wonderful, caring doctor had walked with me on my long journey and demonstrated an abundance of deep respect and concern. It was a joyful miracle for both of us.

God was blessing me with a second chance at embracing life. Like the vulture, who cleans the environment of death and dis-ease, I cleaned my body of the stench and ugliness of Scleroderma in my still fragile and frail body. I couldn't wait to share the news with my parents who had held fast to their belief that God would heal my body. My father had often called late at night when neither of us were able to sleep. We talked and laughed for hours, making up for all the time we lost together when I was a child while he was drinking. He always had a strong faith that something good would come from my illness. He made a point of saying so almost every time we talked.

So it was with great pride that I was finally able to tell my parents the disease was gone. I remember my father's heavy silence upon hearing the news as he stifled his emotion. We were both "weak" that day with tears. A special moment I will always remember sharing with my dad. He was so grateful God had spared his daughter.

When I shared my news with all of my friends on the Internet, I was deluged with congratulations and encouragement. I was pleased to share this blessing of God's miracle that they had helped to create through their constant prayers.

---

[11] To learn more about Sarcoidosis, contact the Sarcoid Networking Association at 253.891.6886 or www.sarcoidsisnetwork.org and request the brochure Facts About Sarcoidosis.

Chapter Twenty Seven
September 11, 2001

"Every blade of grass has its angel that bends over it and whispers 'grow, grow.'"

~ *The Talmud*,
Judaism's holiest book

I am so glad that my father was able to know of my cure from Scleroderma. Because just six days later, Rugged suffered a massive heart attack. It was September 11th.

Like so many war veterans, the savage terrorist attack on America brought back vivid memories and anxiety from earlier days on front lines. My "adopted" sister Tick was critically injured at the Pentagon, saved only because she left her desk to run an errand and was in the hallway of the building when the plane hit her office. The husband of a family friend was on the plane that crashed into the Pentagon. The brother of Gwen Briley-Strand, an actress I know, perished in the World Trade Center. And my uncle Peter, upon learning of his brother's heart attack, had a stroke and landed in a hospital on the other side of town, where 9/11 burn victims like Tick also resided.

So within mere days of my joyful news, the world was plunged into a new and devastating crisis. My mother advised Kim and I not to make the cross-country trek. The airlines might not be safe. Dr. Hillson wouldn't clear me to fly because of an infection. I couldn't afford an airline ticket.

I felt hopeless and helpless and angry that all my joy from the previous week was wiped away by terrorists while my father was hospitalized and dying 3,000 miles away. I cried for two days and mourned him. I thought of the last time I'd left him a few weeks earlier when he'd given me such a strong emotional hug. He'd already been very sick then with a weak heart. I think we both knew it would be our last time together. He often spoke of God's gift to let him live past his assigned time and would often take leave of people by saying, "It was nice knowing you."

Even though I was angry with God that He didn't seem to be helping me get home, I also trusted that, if He could cure the incurable, I would receive what I needed. First I needed to cry and lament my loss. I felt my heart break into tiny pieces as I looked at pictures and listened to my father's favorite music. I was so blessed to have Sheyla at my side the whole time. My friend cried with me as we both prepared ourselves for what was to come next.

The way was made for me to have a ticket gifted to me and my sister. I decided to leave without medical clearance. So we boarded the plane October 1 and I prayed that Mother/Father God would let my father live long enough so that we could say goodbye.

By the time I arrived I was at peace with his leaving. By then I was a second level Reiki practitioner and was able to offer hands on healing to help him make the transition to the afterlife in a peaceful, loving atmosphere. He lit up like a Christmas tree when we arrived and we were blessed to see his joy at being surrounded by his five children.

It was difficult to watch him suffer and wither away to a former shadow of himself. It seemed so cruel. After witnessing the last weeks of his life, I can better appreciate the nickname that he gave himself: Rugged. It was the right name. I often wondered if he had made a deal with God and traded his life for mine or if he waited for my healing before he allowed himself to die.

He held on until November 28 at 6:50 p.m. God answered my prayer and allowed me to be present with him when he died. My niece, Yendi, was singing sweetly to him when he expired as we cried and kissed him goodbye. We watched a blue light cast itself over his body as he went soaring home to God.

I surprised myself with the strength I found inside after Rugged died, especially since the ten week vigil had drained my mind, body, and spirit. At his funeral, there was a great outpouring of love and a church packed with people who came to pay their respects to my father on a Wednesday workday. I miss him but feel his spirit around me. We will always be connected by love.

When I was a young girl, I didn't see a lot of tenderness between my parents. But as an adult, I did witness their strong bond. This strong bond kept them together for more than 50 years. I view my parents as the diamond and pearl of my life.

Many special people came to be with me at my father's funeral. Willie was there and gave an eloquent speech. Sam attended and was very supportive. But most importantly, Kenney showed up.

I realized I was growing tired of our game of cat and mouse over the past three years. He'd say he was still in love with me so I'd work hard to stay in touch while he dated other people and kept busy with his two teenage sons, music, work and pursuing his doctorate.

When I'd returned earlier in October 2001 to be with my sick father, Kenney called frequently but we never got together. So I was elated when I looked up at my father's funeral and saw him there. Afterwards, I teased him by introducing him to family and friends as my husband. He gave a sheepish grin but seemed to enjoy the idea as much as I did.

We verbally expressed our love to each other once again and made plans to have dinner at his mother's home. But just before I was expecting his sisters to pick me up, he called and canceled. I felt he was obsessing about my college boyfriend Willie. Despite my assurances of love and loyalty, I finally realized he didn't believe I wasn't dating anyone or that I'd been celibate for over five years. He didn't seem to trust me or any other woman for that matter.

It was the ultimate test for me to finally recognize that perhaps we were not meant to be. He'd been hurt by too many women. He could no longer trust. I knew now that no matter how much I wanted him in my life, successful relationships must be built on a solid foundation of trust. So I let go and released him from my life. In the end, it was sad but simple.

I realize now I held on to Kenney for far too long. It was always I who was reaching for him, trying to shut out the reality of our diverging paths and different lives. Perhaps I was reaching for that wonderful feeling I felt when I was with him when I was twenty-one, at the prime of my healthy youth.

Now I wish Kenney a life full of love, abundance and prosperity. I will always love him for the gifts he gave me then and now. Once I released my need for him, I was blessed with the freedom to finally love again. I opened my heart and it didn't take long to attract someone special into my life.

So while both my father and Kenney are no longer with me , I now celebrate a new love, my own diamond, in my life at last.

Was it mere coincidence that this old schoolmate happened to be on assignment for work in Seattle in January 2002 and would feel driven to find me through my childhood friend, Denise? As comedian Steve Harvey says, "When you believe in God, unbelievable things can happen to you." This incredible man cares for me and loves me in my present state. My illness does not scare him. He is proud of my accomplishments and courage in winning my battle with Scleroderma. In fact, for him, I am more than Good Enough.

Chapter Twenty Eight
Stop, Drop, and Roll

"You must be the change you wish to see in the world."

~ Mahatma Gandhi

I think one of the most important things I did during my journey into healing was to "stop, drop, and roll"... a formula that belongs to the fire department. I was on fire with dis-ease and had to take immediate action.

I stopped all things that did not serve me mentally, physically, emotionally or spiritually... like my dead-end job at the hospital, toxic people in my life, being the enabler in my family. I no longer allowed these things. I even stopped most activities for a while because I was just too sick. I stopped playing with my life and started praying for it instead.

I had to drop old habits and beliefs in favor of new ways of doing things. I had to drop drama in my life because being at peace is more important than being right. I dropped the need to project an image to the world with the stylish clothes and hair that went with it, so I could be true to my authentic self. And I dropped others' expectations of me. Most importantly, I dropped the lie that I was Not Good Enough.

Then I rolled into healing. I became an active self-healer in my new treatment plan with a new lifestyle and mindset. I rolled over to the west coast in search of clean air, even though I'd never lived that far from my parents before. I rolled into a new mission and sense of purpose. I rolled and rolled in pain, in tears, in sorrow, in guilt, in sadness, in hope and finally in healing.

To date, science has not found a cure for Scleroderma but I have found my healing. Scleroderma taught me so much about myself. I learned how important it is to stop, listen and enjoy the music of life.

Celebrate yourself and find the joy in your life by healing the scars and old wounds of your past. Let your journey into healing take you to a new life filled with infinite possibility.

As you consider my pain, suffering and ultimate triumph, allow my experiences to move you to a higher level of awareness and self-love. Remember: we each have choices to make in our lives. I chose to fight Scleroderma, the dis-ease that threatened to steal my life. But, it saved my life. And for this, I am grateful.

What dis-ease do you need to save your life?

Afterword

As of this writing, I still suffer from Sarcoidosis, another autoimmune dis-ease that I developed along with Scleroderma. Sarcoidosis is considered a multi-system granulomatous dis-ease that can attack any organ of the body and is often caused by viral or bacterial infection, a defective immune system, exposure to toxic substances, or attributed to unknown environmental causes.

In me, this dis-ease continues to affect my lungs. I have been hospitalized only three times since being diagnosed with Sarcoidosis and Scleroderma. I suffer shortness of breath and frequent coughing spells which are helped by medications. And ironically, it includes the steroid, Prednisone! I feel confident that I made the right decision when I refused this medication in the early stages of Scleroderma and also when I elected to use it later. I place strong faith in my intuition. God also continues to grace my life in so many ways, and I believe I will heal from this challenge to my health as well.

One year after Sharon Brinkley penned her poem "Angel with a Broken Wing," I was hospitalized on my birthday. Thousands of miles away, without knowledge of my plight, Sharon was guided towards a figurine on the top shelf of a boutique. To her amazement, it was a beautiful black ceramic angel with a broken wing. I received it from her that day in the hospital and that tender angel watched over me that night.

She does so still from her perch in my bedroom. I touch her each day with love. She reminds me of me. Where I have been and where I can go. She lets me know every day that it is okay to be broken because it is often then, that I can best let go and allow God's grace to work in my life. Being broken is not so bad when I am enveloped by divine love and I know that the cure is in the healing.

Overcome

Dear Father/MotherGod,

You have no idea how much love I am feeling now.

So many lessons, with so much pain.
I can see now it was not in vain.

The sweet rewards are coming fast,
Happiness and health are mine at last.

I worked so hard to reach this goal,
Now there is a chance for me to grow old.

God, you healed me like you said you would.
You found my cure, as only You could.

The tears I've shed filled an ocean bed.
Patience, my child, you often said.

The choice was mine to live or die.
I'm glad I lived and you know why.

To spread the news that You are good,
And faithful to Your word.

Let others know I've overcome.
Flying high like a long-winged bird.

Thank You for the love lessons that Scleroderma taught me,
...for the people that Scleroderma brought me.

Thank You for the healing that Scleroderma sent me.
... for the cure that Scleroderma left me.

Valerie A. Yarborough
January 2003

American Autoimmune-Related Diseases Association (AARDA) is dedicated to the eradication of autoimmune diseases and the alleviation of suffering and the socioeconomic impact of autoimmunity through fostering and facilitating collaboration in the areas of education, research, and patient services.
22100 Gratiot Ave. Eastpointe, E. Detroit, MI 48021
Tel. 586.776.3900, Website: www.aarda.org

American Lung Association was founded in 1904 to fight Tuberculosis, but today fights all forms of lung disease. 61 Broadway, 6th Floor, NY, NY 10006
Tel. 212.315.8700, Website: www.lungusa.org

Dogs for the Disabled is a non-profit organization that trains service dogs for individuals living with Scleroderma.
Email: alfsdogs@charter.net
http:/members.aol.com/Alfs Dogs/

Acupuncture ~ Visit www.acuxo.com for a wide range of acupuncture information, referral and national acupuncture association resources.

American Naturopathic Association ~ Visit www.naturalhealth.org for information on the history natural healing.

National Suicide Prevention Hotlines are available in every state. Live counselors are standing by to speak with you when you feel you can't go on or are in emotional crisis.
Visit http://suicidehotlines.com.

Scleroderma Foundation is a national not-for profit organization with a three-fold mission: (1) to provide social support for Scleroderma victims and their families/friends, (2) education for greater public awareness, and (3)

research about the disease.
12 Kent Way, Suite 101, Byfield, MA 01922
Tel. 800.722.HOPE, Website: www.scleroderma.org

Scleroderma Research Foundation is an organization exclusively dedicated to finding a cure for Scleroderma. SRF's main focus is on funding an innovative research program designed to meet this goal.
2320 Bath Street, Suite 315, Santa Barbara, CA 93105
Website: www.srfcure.org

Scleroderma Wings of Angels Foundation is a non-profit organization dedicated to addressing the social and financial needs of Scleroderma victims and their families through donations and contributions to individuals.
PO Box 1953, Milton, WA, 98354
Tel. 253.952.9387, Website: www.swoaf.org

Human Dimensions ~ Tuangels in Sedona is an organization dedicated to spiritual healing and expansion of the human consciousness through spiritual growth. It provides a structured, safe, and supportive environment by offering nourishing retreats, which allow for growth and healing.
PO Box 559, Sedona AZ 86339
Tel. 928.204.1490, Website: www.tuangels.com

The Road Back Foundation promotes education about the treatment of rheumatic and some connective tissue diseases with low doses of antibiotics; serves as a patient and physician clearinghouse for the exchange and dissemination of information on research and the advances in treatment using such therapy. It supports such research and advocates for these objectives.
PO Box 447, Orleans, MA 02653
Website: www.roadback.org

Recommended Reading

A Set Back is a Set Up for a Comeback by Willie Jolley
All The Joy You Can Stand by Debrena Jackson Gandy
Change Your Life In 30 Days by Rhonda Britten
Depression: It's Ok to Cry by Marianne Williamson
Eight Weeks to Optimum Health by Andrew Weil
Living Better: Every Patient's Guide to Living with Illness by Carol J Langerfeld
One Day My Soul Just Opened Up by Iyanla Vanzant
Scleroderma: A New Role for Patients and Families by Michael Brown
Scleroderma: The Proven Therapy That Can Save Your Life by Henry Scammell
Scleroderma Book, The by Maureen D Mayes
Systemic Sclerosis by Philip J Clements and Daniel E Furst
Michael Brown
Vital Energy: The 7 Keys to Invigorate Body, Mind and Soul by David Simon
Why People Don't Heal by Caroline Myss
You Can Heal Your Life by Louise Hay

Scleroderma **Wings of Angels** Foundation

The Cure is in the Healing... The Scleroderma Wings Of Angels Foundation (SWOAF) is a charitable non-profit organization providing services, support, and social outlets for those affected by scleroderma. We are on a mission of T.E.A.R.S, To Educate All Regarding Scleroderma.

Scleroderma is a rare dis-ease that does not have the same level of exposure and recognition as other life threatening dis-eases. SWOAF is working to raise awareness to provide individualized assistance for victims of scleroderma and their families.

We gladly accept cash donations, volunteer help, in kind donations, and gift certificates. To learn about the many ways you can help and more about our organization, please contact us at 253.952.9387 or visit us at www.swoaf.org.

Thank Yous

First and foremost I thank Father/Mother God for giving me the gift of this life, and the opportunity to share my miracle of divine healing with the world. I have been given a second chance and am so very grateful. Special thanks and love to all the individuals, families, organizations, churches and religions that helped me on my journey.

My beloved parents Baxter and Virginia, (a.k.a. Rugged and Miss Daisy Doodle) family and friends especially Angela Jones, Azarel Smallwood, Baltazar Soto, Cascade Park Gardens, Dale Perry, Dr. Eric Henderson, HyunSook Chung, Jamel Covington Taborn, Juliah Barker, Lady Nellie Thompson, Nan Dunston, Rita Ravin, and Tony Hudson

About the Author

A native of Washington DC, Valerie A. Yarborough currently resides in Washington State. Founder and active member of The Scleroderma Wings Of Angels Foundation (SWOAF), she is currently working on creative projects which include writing, singing, and public speaking.